MW01140725

A Phonology, Morphology, and Classified Word List for the Samish Dialect of Straits Salish

Brent D. Galloway

Canadian Ethnology Service
Mercury Series Paper 116

Canadian Museum of Civilization

© Canadian Museum of Civilization 1990

Canadian Cataloguing in Publication Data

Galloway, Brent Douglas

A phonology, morphology, and classified word list
for the Samish dialect of Straits Salish

(Mercury series, ISSN 0316-1854)
(Paper / Canadian Ethnology Service,
ISSN 0316-1862 ; no. 116)
Includes an abstract in French.
Includes bibliographical references.
ISBN 0-660-10799-6

1. Salish language. 2. Coast Salish Indians –
Languages. 3. Indians of North America – British
Columbia – Languages. I. Canadian Museum of
Civilization. II. Canadian Ethnology Service. III.
Title. IV. Series: Paper (Canadian Ethnology
Service); no. 116.

PM2263.G34 1990   497'.9   C90-098566-6

Printed and bound in Canada

Published by the
Canadian Museum of Civilization
100 Laurier Street
P.O. Box 3100, Station B
Hull, Quebec
J8X 4H2

Canadian Ethnology Service
Papers Coordinator:
Pamela Coulas

Canadä

OBJECT OF THE MERCURY SERIES

The Mercury Series is designed to permit the rapid
dissemination of information pertaining to the
disciplines in which the Canadian Museum of
Civilization is active. Considered an important
reference by the scientific community, the Mercury
Series comprises over three hundred specialized
publications on Canada's history and prehistory.

Because of its specialized audience, the series
consists largely of monographs published in the
language of the author.

In the interest of making information available
quickly, normal production procedures have been
abbreviated. As a result, grammatical and
typographical errors may occur. Your indulgence is
requested

Titles in the Mercury Series can be obtained by
writing to:

> Mail Order Services
> Publishing Division
> Canadian Museum of Civilization
> 100 Laurier Street
> P.O. Box 3100, Station B
> Hull, Quebec
> J8X 4H2

BUT DE LA COLLECTION MERCURE

La collection Mercure vise à diffuser rapidement le
résultat de travaux dans les disciplines qui relèvent
des sphères d'activités du Musée canadien des
civilisations. Considérée comme un apport
important dans la communauté scientifique, la
collection Mercure présente plus de trois cents
publications spécialisées portant sur l'héritage
canadien préhistorique et historique.

Comme la collection s'adresse à un public spécialisé
celle-ci est constituée essentiellement de
monographies publiées dans la langue des auteurs.

Pour assurer la prompte distribution des exemplaires
imprimés, les étapes de l'édition ont été abrégées.
En conséquence, certaines coquilles ou fautes de
grammaire peuvent subsister : c'est pourquoi nous
réclamons votre indulgence.

Vous pouvez vous procurer la liste des titres parus
dans la collection Mercure en écrivant au :

> Service des commandes postales
> Division de l'édition
> Musée canadien des civilisations
> 100, rue Laurier
> C.P. 3100, succursale B
> Hull (Québec)
> J8X 4H2

Abstract

This volume presents a description of the phonology and morphology of the Samish dialect of the Straits Salish language, together with a text and word list, classified by semantic domain, of the same language. The preface discusses the precarious survival of this little-documented dialect through the movement of two families from their homeland in the vicinity of Anacortes, Washington and adjacent islands to Vancouver Island in British Columbia.

Résumé

Ce volume présente une description de la phonologie et la morphologie du samish, un dialecte du straits salish, accompagnée d'un texte et d'une liste de mots, classés selon la sémantique de la même langue. Dans l'avant-propos, l'auteur traite de la survivance précaire de ce dialecte mal connu à travers le déplacement de deux familles de leur habitat aux environs d'Anacortes et des îles avoisinantes, dans l'état de Washington, à l'île de Vancouver en Colombie-Britannique.

Les personnes désireuses de recevoir en français de plus amples renseignements sur cette publication sont priées d'adresser leur demande au :

Service canadien d'ethnologie
Musée canadien des civilisations
C.P. 3100, Succ. B
Hull (Québec)
J8X 4H2

CONTENTS

In December of 1983 I was contacted by Dr. Jay Powell of the Department of Anthropology, University of British Columbia. He invited me to join him and Ken Hansen, Chairman of the Samish Tribe, in a discussion of the possibility of linguistic fieldwork with a speaker of the Samish dialect of Straits Salish. This was exciting news because the Samish dialect was thought to have become extinct 20 or even 30 years ago; no tapes were known to have been made of this dialect and only a small sample of words had been transcribed (circa 1948 by Wayne Suttles).

The Straits language (or Straits Salish) was aboriginally spoken by peoples along the north shore of the Olympic Peninsula from Clallam Bay to Port Discovery (Clallam) and by peoples on the San Juan and Gulf Islands between Washington and Vancouver Island (Strait of Juan de Fuca and Strait of Georgia) and adjacent coastlines. It was and is spoken in both the state of Washington and the province of British Columbia. It now comprises two languages, Northern Straits and Clallam (most consider these separate languages). Northern Straits includes the following dialects: Sooke, Songish, Saanich, Lummi, and Samish. Semiahmoo may have also been a Northern Straits dialect, but only a few early short word lists survive (for ex. Gibbs ca 1853–1860). Samish speakers aboriginally "dominated a cluster of islands around Samish and Guemes Islands" (Thompson, Thompson and Efrat 1974:184), probably including Samish, Guemes, Cypress, Burrows, Allen, Blakely, Decatur, and part of Lopez, San Juan and Fidalgo Islands.

In 1951 Wayne Suttles completed an excellent ethnography of the Straits people as his Ph.D. dissertation, "Economic Life of the Coast Salish of Haro and Rosario Straits". This includes ethnographic information on the Samish and some Samish names and words are cited. Suttles reported working with Charlie Edwards, "probably the last speaker of the Samish dialect", who died in Dec. 1948 and Annie Lyons, a partial speaker of Samish. Chafe 1962 reported approximately two speakers of Samish then alive in Washington, as part of his report on estimates of speakers of North American Indian languages. The only linguistic material available on Samish, besides the handful in Suttles 1951, is that in Thompson, Thompson and Efrat 1974 (two words, and perhaps nine more quoted as being the same in all Northern Straits dialects). Until 1983 linguists had thought that the last speakers of Samish were dead.

Ken Hansen, chairman of the Samish Tribe, headquartered in Anacortes, Washington, on Fidalgo Island, had learned of a man living in British Columbia who still spoke Samish fluently. He and anthropologist Sally Snyder interviewed him in 1983 and recorded a Samish text, The Maiden of Deception Pass, from him. He was indeed fluent and speaks both the

Saanich dialect and the Samish dialect fluently at winter ceremonies
and spirit dances. I was free to work with him until Sept. 1984 if
funding could be found for the field work. I quickly applied for an
urgent ethnography contract with the Canadian Ethnology Service at the
National Museum of Man in Ottawa, to tape record and analyze whatever
Samish material I could obtain in 25 days, six-hour sessions each day.
The contract was approved and the Samish tribe also found some funds
to help out. I would like to express my deep gratitude to both the
Canadian Ethnology Service and the Samish Tribe for their timely
support of this project.

   I began work with Victor Underwood Sr. of the Tsawout Reserve, East
Saanich, Vancouver Island, British Columbia. Born on Orcas Island in
Washington, he had learned Samish from his grandfather, David Tom,
and Saanich from his grandmother, Cecilia (Sam) Tom; Victor's mother
died shortly after he was born (about 1914), and his grandparents raised
him on Orcas and Guemes Islands. In about 1928 Victor left Orcas Island
and stayed in Anacortes. When he was about 16 he came to East Saanich where
he lives on land inherited from his grandmother. He never spoke English
till he left Orcas Island. In 1935 he married Ethel, a fluent speaker
of the Cowichan dialect of Halkomelem (and of English). Victor has
learned some Cowichan and some Lummi as well as being a fluent speaker
of English; Ethel understands Saanich and Samish also.

   We began on July 11, 1984 by re—eliciting the only traditional story
that Victor remembers completely in Samish, the story of qʷəɫásəɫwət,
the maiden of Deception Pass. I then began elicited Samish words cognate
with words I had in the other Straits dialects in publications and
manuscripts. As we worked Victor was sometimes unsure whether a
particular form he remembered was in the Samish dialect or in the
Saanich dialect. After Victor had given me a few such terms he suggested
that he should check them out with his "aunt" (his grandfather's sister's
child), Mrs. Lena Daniels, on the Malahat Reserve, also on Vancouver Island.
He said she is also fluent in Samish, in fact has never spoken anything
else. At this pleasant surprise I encouraged him to try to contact her
if he could. We continued work the rest of the week, marking any forms
Victor was unsure of.

   On July 16th Victor had found out where to reach his aunt, and he phoned
her to ask if the three of us could meet and work together. With Victor's
permission I recorded his end of the phone conversation, which was all in
Samish. Mrs. Daniels was interested and on July 24th took a ferry to
the Saanich peninsula, Victor drove her to his house, and we spent a very
productive day checking and eliciting forms. Thereafter she joined us
for almost all the remaining sessions. We met most weekdays through August

24, 1984, then were not able to resume our sessions till June 10, 1985. We finished the funded work June 19, 1985, toward the end getting seven stories told in Samish by Mrs. Daniels.

In our joint sessions I would give an English word, phrase or sentence, Victor would give a definition in Samish to Lena, they would discuss it in Samish, then Lena would give the Samish form several times, followed by Victor. In many cases Victor knew the word and gave it first, but we always recorded Lena's pronunciation as well. One ground rule was that to avoid influence from other dialects I would only prompt with a form from another dialect after Victor (and Lena) had taken all the time they wanted to try to remember the Samish form. They were quite conscientious. In turn, I tried to pick up as much conversational Samish as I could, to use in eliciting.

Lena Daniels understands some English (if spoken slowly) but can speak very very little. She understands the Cowichan dialect of Halkomelem quite well and speaks a little more of it than English but is not fluent. We had two sessions with Ethel Underwood explaining what I was asking in Cowichan and Lena replying in Samish. This in fact is how the two of them usually communicate. Lena was born on the Malahat Reserve (where Cowichan is the Indian language normally spoken). She is about the same age as Victor, perhaps a year or two older. She was born Madeline Harry, daughter of Cecilia Tom (1866-1949) and Harry Steel (1858-1949). Cecilia was a sister of Victor's grandfather David Tom (1850/56-1940) and spoke fluent Samish. Harry Steel (also known as Steel Harry) was Cowichan and spoke Cowichan.

Intrigued by finding this degree of fluency in transplanted families when the language had died out in the United States, I asked, through Victor, how Lena had kept up her Samish and whom she had talked with. Lena's mother had spoken only Samish to her children; they all became fluent speakers of Samish with her (till her death about 1949) and with each other. Lena spoke only Samish to her children, several of whom can still speak Samish (though their children speak only English). Lena's sister, Emma taught all of her children Samish; one is still alive at Malahat in his late 50's and still fluent. One of Emma's daughters had a son who can speak Samish. Others of Cecilia and Harry Steel's grandchildren learned Samish but only speak Cowichan now. So within this extended family, Samish has been moved to Vancouver Island and has precariously survived. What is unclear is how fluent the younger generation of speakers is (there are three who are said to speak Samish and two more who may also speak it or may just understand it). Victor's children can understand some Samish but do not speak it.

One further attestation of Samish has come to light. Mrs. Violet

Hilbert, t̲áqʷšəblu, a speaker, teacher and researcher of the Lushootseed
language at the University of Washington in Seattle, has been transcri-
bing some Lushootseed tapes made in the early 1950's by Leon Metcalf.
They are now in the University of Washington archives. One tape (#20)
is an interview in October 1952 with Tommy Bob speaking in Samish.
Mrs. Hilbert kindly made the tape available to me in 1985 to copy,
transcribe, and play for Victor and Lena. It includes most of the
Swadesh 200-word list (Tommy Bob gives 149 words). Then Tommy Bob gives
a medium sized text of about 50 or so lines in a formal speech style.
This material really rounds out the samples of Samish speech (citation,
conversation, stories, speeches). It also gives attestation to an older
generation of Samish as Tommy Bob died in the 1950's. He lived at
LaConner, Wash. on the Swinomish Reserve, as did a number of Samish.
His mother and Victor's grandmother were sisters.

One other helpful step in the present fieldwork was a trip to Orcas
Island, Washington organized by Ken Hansen. Joining us there were Victor
and Ethel Underwood, Mrs. Lena Daniels, Mrs. Laura Edwards (speaker of the
Skagit dialect of Lushootseed), Wayne Suttles, anthropologist Sally Snyder,
and tribal secretary Mrs. Mary Hansen. The first day we worked on Samish
with Wayne Suttles confirming that it sounded like the true Samish he had
heard years ago in his work. We also did mutual intelligibility tests
and comparative elicitation with Samish, Saanich, Skagit, and several
dialects of Halkomelem, as well as some ethnographic elicitation. The
second day we chartered a boat to round parts of Orcas Island to elicit
place names, ethnographic information, and marine terms in Samish.

My goal has been to gather enough material for a preliminary analysis
of the phonology and some morphology with as full a citation of data as
possible, including an index or word list and some sentence examples.
To benefit from previous linguistic work on other Straits dialects I
elicited forms cognate with forms in previous works, for example:
Suttles 1951, Thompson, Thompson and Efrat 1974, Demers 1974, Raffo 1972,
Charles, Demers and Bowman 1978, Efrat 1969, Galloway 1977, Demers p.c.
1982, Galloway 1982, Bouchard 1974, Galloway 1980, U.S. Census 1880,
Kennedy 1974 ms., Thompson and Thompson 1971, and Montler 1984. Other
work which was helpful was Mitchell 1968, Pidgeon 1970, Thompson 1972,
Demers 1980a and 1980b, and Jelinek and Demers 1983.

It may be of interest here to mention Victor Underwood's impression
that the Samish dialect is most similar to the Lummi dialect, then next
most similar to the Saanich dialect. This seems likely for geographic
reasons and may well be confirmed by the present data, but there has not
yet been time to study this fully.

One final word here. The Samish and Saanich people I have met have
all been friendly and very supportive of this work. It has been a pleasure
to work with them. I look forward to more work with them in the future.

Dedicated to the Memory of Victor Underwood

who passed away August 1988

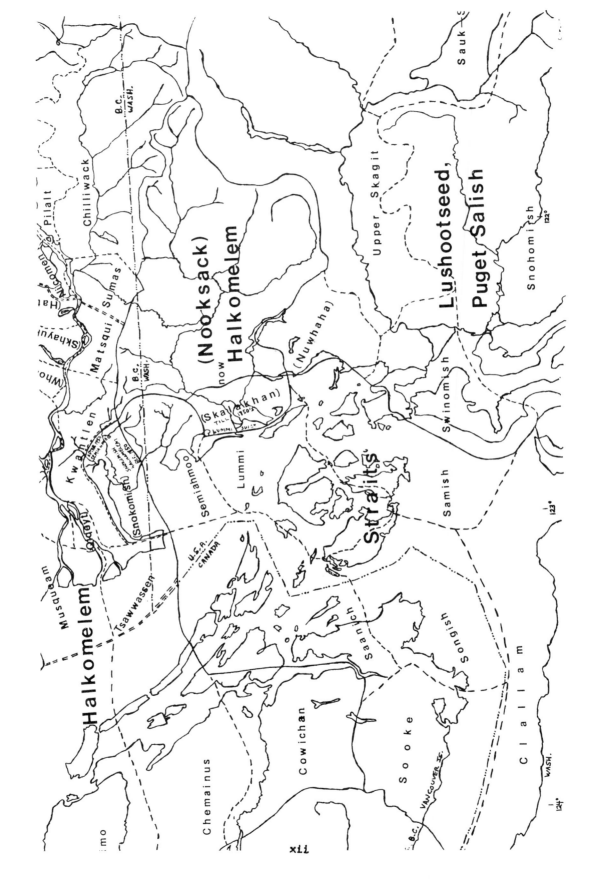

1. PHONEMICS

1.0. SAMISH PHONEMES

	Bilab.	Inter-Dental	Apico-Alveolar			Pal.	Velar		Postvelar		Glottal
			sl.	lat.	gr.		plain	lab.	plain	lab.	
Obstruents											
plain	p		t (c)		č	(k)	kʷ	q	qʷ	?	
glottalized	ṗ	ɵ̇	t̓ (c̓)	ƛ̓	č̓		k̓ʷ	q̓	q̓ʷ		
Spirants			s	ł	š		xʷ	x̣	x̣ʷ	h	
Resonants											
plain	m		n	l	y		w	ŋ			
glottalized	ṁ		ṅ	l̓	ẏ		ẇ	ŋ̓			
Vowels											
high					i		(u)				
mid					e	ə					
low						a					
Suprasegmentals											
stress											
length											

(sl. = slit, gr. = groove, lat. = lateral, lab. = labialized, pal. = palatal)

Comments on the chart:

1. /c/ is very rare, occuring only in the deictic morpheme (cə). However, this morpheme is fairly common and is also combines with some suffixes to form deictic pronouns, etc. Historically it is a mere combination of t + s (each of whose functions can be demonstrated).

2. /k/ is found only in loan words from European languages (English, French) and Chinook Jargon.

3. [c̓] is quite common in VU's pronunciation but corresponds to /ɵ̇/ in the speech of LD and TB. While LD's speech could have conceivably been influenced by the Cowichan Halkomelem /ɵ̇/, it seems unlikely that TB's speech was (he did not live in a Cowichan speaking area). TB had some Saanich ancestors but did not live in a Saanich speaking area, so it seems unlikely that he was using /ɵ̇/ from Saanich influence. On the other hand, VU grew up on Orcas Island, a Lummi speaking area, and emphasizes the similarity of Lummi to Samish. Thus VU's /c̓/ could be influence from Lummi (which has /c̓/, not /ɵ̇/). It could also be influence from Saanich which VU grew up speaking since Saanich /ɵ̇/ is more often pronounced [t̓ˢ] than [ɵ̇] (see Montler 1984:8-9 and see below). Since the two older speakers have /ɵ̇/, it seems more likely that Samish in their day had /ɵ̇/ rather than /c̓/. None of the speakers of Samish use both, and none of the other dialects of Straits tolerate both /c̓/ and /ɵ̇/, so Samish was very unlikely to have both.

4. /u/ is found mainly in loan words from Indian and European languages

as well as from Chinook Jargon. There may be a few cases also where /w/
has become vocalized recently to /u/ or where the combination /əw/ sounds
very close to [u] in closed syllables (though [əw] is more frequent).
5. /m/ and /m̓/ are evidently not restricted to loans.

1.1. DESCRIPTION OF PHONETICS AND ALLOPHONES

1.1.1. Obstruents

   Stops are unaspirated in the following positions: S_V, _R(#,C), #_R
where S = spirant, V = vowel, R = resonant, (#,C) = pause or consonant
(resonants in these positions are syllabic).

Thus (all citations by VU and LD unless preceded by speaker's initials):
[kʷm̓ʔstəlíʔq̓ʷ] 'mushroom'
[skʷíɖən] ~ [skʷíqŋ], TB [skʷéɖən] 'flower'
[sʔásəs·#ƛ̓ənʔ#séləs] 'palm of your hand'
[sqə́maʔ̓] 'breast, nipple; milk'
VU [stéˆskʷəɬ], LD [stéˆskʷɬ], TB [stæskʷəɬ] 'back (anatomy)'
[spəƛ̓ínəs] 'chest-bone (of bird for ex.)'
[sqʷáʔtn̩] 'bucket'
[qʷlá·ysəƛ̓ən?] 'phonograph, record player'
VU [štə́ŋ] 'to walk'
[šqənxʷélə] 'inside throat, gullet'
[šqʷəné̓ˆləɖ̓sən] 'hair in the nose'
[štələháləs] 'eyeglasses'
VU [léŋnənɬtə] 'he sees us (lit. we are seen)'
VU, TB [sʔáɬqəʔ̓] 'snake'
VU [səɬtéˇlŋuxʷ] ~ (faster) [sɬtéˇlŋuxʷ], LD [sɬtéˇlənuxʷ] 'whole body'
LD, TB [ɬqét̓] 'clothes, dress'
[šxʷʔíləχən] 'side of the body (human or animal)'
VU [xʷqéyəχqən?], LD (correcting) [q̓éyəχqé?nəŋ?] 'tell(ing) a made-up
 story', TB [q̓ə̓yəχqn̩] 'to lie'
VU [ċə́χtən(ʔ)], LD [θ́əχtn̩] 'poison' (t ~ t̓)
VU [ċəχtən?ít̓], LD [θ́əχtən?nít̓] 'to poison s-o' (t ~ t̓)
TB [p̓kʷ̓ǽtn̩] 'flow'
TB [ʔánəstən] 'given'
TB [ʔǽɬti] 'here' (t clear and unaspirated)
(Note: glottalized resonants are almost always realized as resonant plus
an adjacent unaspirated glottal stop. See below under resonants.)

   /ʔ/ is optionally aspirated only V_(V,#); it is unreleased _C
and often C_# (where C = consonant).

Thus besides examples elsewhere:

VU [spč̓á?ʼ] 'watertight basket' (?ʰ ~ ?)
VU [səsí?lə?ʼ] 'grandmother'
VU [léʔʼɛ] 'there' (?ʰ ~ ?)

Elsewhere stops are aspirated (LD's final stops often weakly aspirated).

Besides some of the examples above, the following show such aspiration:
[t̓éčsṇ], TB [t̓ə́čsṇ] 'back of neck, back of head'
[q̓ə́lən?], TB [q̓ə́lən] 'eye'
TB [p̓áxʷət̓] 'blow (like of the wind)'
TB [t̓ək̓ʷuxʷ], VU [t̓ək̓ʷuxʷ] 'nine'
VU [lək̓əlí] 'key' (loan from Chinook Jargon < French le clef)
VU [xʷlək̓əlít̓] 'to lock something'
VU [p̓q̓ʷéčən], TB [p̓q̓ʷéčṇ] 'sand'
VU [sq̓p̓íq̓ʷəs], LD [sq̓p̓íq̓ʷs] 'white hanging lichen (grows on alder)'
VU [q̓t̓əlí?q̓ʷ], LD [šq̓ət̓əlí?q̓ʷ](q̓ʷ has weak aspiration) 'top of
 head, crown of head'
VU [lisék̓t̓] 'put it in the sack'
VU [spáp̓ək̓ʷ], LD [spáp̓k̓ʷ] 'lump (on tree, ground, person)'
TB, VU, LD [ŋə́q̓sṇ] 'nose'
TB [sŋǽ·nt̓], VU, LD [sŋénət̓] ~ [sŋé·nt̓] 'rock, mountain'
[t̓sás] 'poor'
VU [č̓ɪlq̓ʷɬnét̓] 'Tuesday'

Geminate obstruents are rearticulated.

Thus, VU [?əmát̓t̓xʷ] 'seat somebody'
LD [?ít̓t̓] 'to sleep'
LD [kʷɬ ?í?t̓t̓] 'still sleeping now'
LD [sŋéˆč̓č̓] 'lagoon', VU [šŋé?č̓əč̓] 'any bay'

This contrasts with geminate spirants and resonants which are subject
to a morphophonemic rule converting the second member to length (/·/).
For example, VU //tsás-sən// /tsás·ən/ [tsás·ən] 'I'm poor',
//s=?ásəs-s t-ən séləs// /s?ásəs· tən séləs/ 'palm of your hand',
//pén=nəxʷ=əŋ// /pén·əxʷəŋ/ [pén·uxʷəŋ] 'Matia Island'.

Glottalized obstruents are fairly fortis in pronunciation. Aspiration,
especially in consonant clusters, is fairly strong also. From this point
on aspiration of stops will not be reproduced in phonetic quotations.

Although Samish has /θ̓/, /ƛ̓/, and in loans, /k/, it lacks plain counter-
parts of the first two and a glottalized counterpart of the last. /θ̓/
is actually a glottalized interdental affricate (thus it is listed among
the obstruents rather than among the spirants). As discussed in the comments

on the table above, /θ̇/ is pronounced roughly as [č̣] by VU but as the interdental affricate by LD and TB. Montler 1984:8-9 mentions a similar but dental
pronunciation is the norm for Saanich. In a number of places my transcription
actually shows VU using a dental [č̣]. The environment for this fronting
does not seem predictable. VU's Saanich forms show the dental norm for both
/θ̇/ and /θ/ as Montler reports for his speakers; (interdental pronunciations
are found but are rare in Saanich). In Samish LD and TB have interdental /θ̇/
only. VU also has interdental /θ̇/ but rarely.

No significant allophony has been noted for the obstruents not mentioned
so far. Examples of minimal and subminimal contrasts of all phonemes will
be given in section 1.2.

1.1.2. Spirants

All three speakers of Samish use an occasional [θ]. These are lapses
as is shown by the facts that they are almost always corrected to [s], that
they sometimes occur for a few citations after EU has been speaking Cowichan
or VU has been speaking Saanich (both of which have /θ/), and that if not
corrected immediately, the forms are attested everywhere else by the same
speaker with [s].

In a number of forms VU has a dental [s̪] where Saanich and Cowichan
have /θ/. Wary that this might indicate a phonemic contrast between dental
[s̪] and alveolar [s], I checked very carefully as I elicited. LD uses only
alveolar [s] in both cases (where Cowichan and Saanich have /s/ and where they
have /θ/). TB has examples both of [θ] and dental [s̪] (usually the first
corrected to the second) where Saanich has /θ/, and of alveolar [s] (where
Saanich has /θ/ and where it has /s/). VU has the dental [s̪] for Saanich
(as he should) and even occasionally in a Cowichan word (where he should
have [θ]). Both VU and LD have words in which a root ending in [s] in
Samish, Cowichan, and Saanich) precedes a suffix beginning with [s]
in Samish but /θ/ in Cowichan and Saanich; in these cases both VU and LD
are able to use the morphophonemic rule which changes the second member
of a geminate cluster to /·/. Thus Samish [snás·ət], Cowichan [náseθət]
'get fat'. This rule does not apply when Samish [š] and [s] are adjacent.

The most likely conclusion then is that Samish has only one phoneme /s/.
VU and TB sometimes pronounce it as dental [s̪] where Saanich has a
dental [s̪] /θ/ corresponding, and this is Saanich dialect interference.
LD who might be expected to show Cowichan influence does not use the
dental [s̪] precisely because it is Saanich influence, and her family
background does not show a likelihood of Saanich influence like VU's
and TB's.

Some examples include:

VU [θiyəqʷíŋəł] 'dig' but later VU [sáyəqʷt] 'dig it up'

LD [spéˇʔεˆθ] but one page later LD, VU [spéˇʔεˇs] 'bear'

LD [θəwʔníł], VU [cəwʔníł] 'him' (vs. LD, VU [səwʔníł] 'her'), just
 a few citations after Cowichan citations by EU (Cowichan would use
 [tθ] in the same rare deictics where Samish has [c])

VU [kʷél?əgət], LD [kʷél?əst] 'tip (oneself over) in a canoe' (with
 a suffix cognate to Cow. (-θət/)

VU [s?ágəs] ~ [s?ásəs], LD [s?ásəs], (Cow., Saan. /s?áθəs/) 'face'

VU, LD [šxʷsécs], EU Cow. [sčépθ] 'uncle or aunt by marriage' (note
 that Samish /šxʷ-/ is a nominalizer as is Cow. /s-/ and that the
 Cow. [č] /c/, /p/, and /θ/ respectively correspond historically to
 the Samish /s/, /č/, and /s/)(Thompson, Thompson, and Efrat 1974,
 Raffo 1972, and Galloway 1982)

VU [?ə́čəqsət] ~ [?ə́čəqsət], LD [?ə́čəqst] 'move oneself, get out
 of the way, go off to the side' (Upriver Halkomelem has
 /?íyəqθət/ 'dodge, get out of the way')

LD Samish = EU Cow. [s?iy?aləmíw?s] 'right side of body'

LD, VU [séˆščən], TB [θæ̆ščən] corrected to [sæ̆ščən] 'blood'

TB [θáθən] corrected to [sáθən], LD, VU [sásən] 'mouth'

TB [θx̣ə́t], corrected to [sx̣ə́t] 'push, shove s-o or s-th'

TB [?áyæθ], LD, VU [?áya?s], Saan. (Montler 1984:87) //?ə́y=əθ//
 '(it's) sharped-edged'

VU [kʷés·ət] 'it's getting warmer' (compare Upriver Halkomelem
 /k̓ʷásəət/ 'get warm')

VU [šsəłqʷíŋ?əł], LD [səłqʷíŋ?əł] 'awl' (VU, LD [sə́łqʷ] 'a hole')

No significant allophony has been found for the remaining spirants
in Samish. For example, in some other dialects of Straits /ł/ is
reported to have an occasional affricated allophone, [ƛ]. Such an
allophone has not been found in Samish. Examples of all spirant
phonemes will be found, with contrasts, in section 1.2.

1.1.3. Resonants

Samish has a matched set of plain and glottalized resonants. The glottalized resonants appear to have arisen historically from clusters of glottal stop plus resonant, probably encouraged by a morphophonemic rule inherited from Proto-Central Salish which inserts glottal stop adjacent to resonants to mark 'continuative' (= 'actual') aspect in verbs. Glottalized resonants in Samish almost always decompose phonetically into clusters of plain resonant plus glottal stop; there are only a handful of examples of words pronounced with phonetic glottalized resonants as a variant. More on this below.

Samish /ŋ/ and /ŋ̓/ are post-velar nasals rather than velar ones. They are articulated in the same position as Samish /q/, /q̓/, and /x̣/. This was first described for a Straits dialect by Thompson (1972:257) for Lummi, where Lummi /ŋ/ is listed as a uvular resonant in the same column with /q, q̓, x̣/. It was hinted at by Raffo (1972:7,11) for Songish, but Songish /ŋ/ was still said to be velar, though "very back" and thus the resonant counterpart of /x̣/. Montler (1984:18) is the clearest in this regard for Saanich: "/ŋ/ and /ŋ̓/ are post-velar, usually produced farther toward the back of the soft palate than the velar nasal in English 'lung'." Clallam and Sooke are described as having a velar /ŋ/.

/m/ is historically related to /ŋ/. In Samish it is less common than /ŋ/ but it is not rare. /n, n̓, l, l̓/ are all articulated as apico-alveolar resonants. /y/ and /y̓/ are articulated as medio-palatal resonants. /w/ and /w̓/ are articulated as labio-velar resonants and in fact alternate with /kʷ/ morphophonemically and historically.

Glottalized resonants are treated as clusters of plain resonant plus /ʔ/ in the descriptions of Sooke (Efrat 1969), Clallam (Thompson and Thompson 1971), Lummi (Thompson 1972), and Songish (Raffo 1972). Raffo gives six convincing arguments why this is so in Songish and supports each with ample data. Thompson, Thompson and Efrat (1974) and Efrat (1978) examine the situation in Straits and lean toward the view that glottalized resonants may well be phonemic in Straits (Efrat says this may be the case for the Sooke and Saanich dialects). Hukari (1981) concludes that they are phonemic for the Cowichan dialect of Halkomelem (Galloway 1977 and 1982 show that they are not present in Upriver Halkomelem due to loss of /ʔ/ adjacent to consonants). Montler (1984) concludes that glottalized resonants are phonemic in Saanich and gives four convincing arguments why this is so.

Both the arguments or tests of Raffo and Montler can be applied to see what the phonemic status of glottalized resonants in Samish is. Let R = any plain resonant and R' = any glottalized resonant.

1. Raffo found no minimal or even near minimal pairs contrasting R and
R'. Montler found minimal pairs (though only of roots, not of utterances).
I found two apparently minimal pairs, LD, VU [q̓ʷəyíləš] 'dance' and
LD [q̓ʷəy̓íləš], VU [q̓ʷəyíl?əš] 'dancing', and LD [qʷéləst] 'bail oneself' and LD, VU [qʷél?əst] 'boil something', and some minimal roots. But
if clusters are involved one would expect the addition of a phoneme to
make a difference in any case. This is no real help.

2. Raffo found that in Songish neither R? nor ?R are reduplicated as a
unit (as a phoneme would have to be). Thus Songish [qén?] 'to steal'
but [qén?qən] 'thief', [q̓ʷám?] 'strong' but [q̓ʷám?q̓ʷəm] 'very strong',
etc. Montler found however that in Saanich R? and ?R were reduplicated
as units, for example with C₁VC₂+ 'characteristic', C₁C₂+ 'plural', and
C₁C₂+ 'repetitive' reduplications. Thus Saanich /qén/ 'to steal' and
/šqén̓qən̓s/ 'thief', /stáləw̓/ 'river' and /stəl̓táləw̓/ 'rivers',
/?én̓/ 'much' and /?ən̓?én̓/ 'too much'. In Samish both R? and ?R are
reduplicated as units. Thus Samish has:
[qén?] 'to steal' and VU [qén?qən?] 'thief'
[k̓ʷám?k̓ʷəm?] 'strong'
[stá?ləw?] 'river' and [stəl?tá?ləw?] 'rivers'
[?éˇ?ləŋ] 'house' and [é?lɛˇ?ləŋ?] 'houses'
[sxʷáy?ɪł] 'awake' and [sxʷəy?xʷəy?] 'lively'

3. Raffo found that in Songish glottal release was heard before and
after R in these clusters but she never heard glottalization co-articulated
with R. Montler found for Saanich that R' was heard with glottalization
co-articulated and creaky voice (laryngeal tension) in monosyllables;
in polysyllablic words R' normally decomposed to ?R phonetically in the
environment V´_V and to R? phonetically in the environment V_V´. However,
he found this was optional and that in those positions and elsewhere
?R and R? both varied with R enunciated with creaky voice. Montler found
that in Saanich decomposition of R' was sporadic but had phonetic justi-
fication: laryngeal tension carried over from a stressed vowel gives
[?] a headstart and conversely is carried over to a following stressed
vowel from an R' preceding. In the case of Samish, I found co-articulation
of resonant and glottalization extremely rare but present (decomposition
is the rule). Here are all of the examples I have found to date of true
co-articulated glottalized resonants:
VU [híwəl? ~ hí?wəl? ~ híw?əl?], LD [hí?wəl] 'go toward, come toward'
VU [siléwtxʷ ~ siléw̓txʷ], LD [siléw̓xʷ] 'tent'
VU [k̓čéwtxʷ ~ k̓čéw̓txʷ], LD [k̓čéw̓xʷ] 'bottom of a house'
 (all three examples within 12 words of each other in one interview may
 indicate that such pronunciations are targets or lapses; however between
 these examples were the more common pronunciations:

LD [čέˆʔləmənéwʔxʷ], VU [čεˆləmənéwʔtxʷ] 'log house')
VU [xʷsiẏáməs], LD [xʷsiyʔáʔməs] 'brave'
LD [ʔínətsxʷə(č)], VU [ʔínətsxʷač] 'what did you say?'
LD, VU [mɛ́lqʷ] 'uvula'
LD [hanáẏɫ] 'lullaby'
LD [seʔéʔwʔəs ~ seʔéẃəs], VU [seʔéʔwəs] 'putting it down'
LD [səwʔwə́yʔqa], VU [səw·ə́yʔqəʔ] 'lots of men'
LD [ɵ̇əčə́lʔləʔ] 'kingfisher'
LD [ɵ̇əx̣tən̓ʔnít], VU [c̓əx̣tən̓ʔít] 'to poison someone'
(Notice that all but three of these examples occurs in the environment
non-finally after a stressed vowel. More on this in paragraph 6 below
in the discussion of the decomposition rule for Samish.)

4. Montler found that ʔR and R' contrast on the morphophonemic level
in at least one rule in Saanich:
'actual aspect' //-ʔ-// infix -> ʔə in the environment V´_ʔ
                              but -> ʔ in the environments V´_R', V_R
Thus Saanich //√ʔəlé[ʔə]ʔ-nəxʷ sən// /ʔəlé?ənəxʷ sən/ 'I'm hearing it now.'
and /ʔəlénəxʷ sən/ 'I heard something.' vs. //kʷɫ √t̓ə[ʔ]m̓-t ɫtə//
/kʷɫ t̓əm̓t ɫtə/ 'I'm hitting him.' and /t̓əm̓ət ɫtə/ 'We hit it.'
I have not yet been able to find comparable forms for Samish, but since
this is a morphophonemic rule it does not really affect the phonemics of
resonants.

5. Raffo suggested several other diachronic factors supporting the
cluster analysis of R' in Songish. These include the facts that
comparative evidence shows: that /ʔ/ has been lost or added historically
in word-final position, that in some cognates /ʔ/ has shifted position
from one syllable adjacent to a resonant in one language to the next
syllable in other languages, and that there are a number of cases of
Songish /ʔ/ adjacent to R in correspondence with Chilliwack Halkomelem
phonemic length just as /ʔ/ adjacent to other consonants is in correspondence with the same Chilliwack Halkomelem phonemic length. It is true
that these facts support the diachronic cluster origin of R', and
all else being equal they would be decisive. They support the case of
Songish, where the other factors point in the direction of clusters.
But in Saanich and Samish the other factors point in the other direction,
so, as Montler points out, diachronic factors are less relevant than
synchronic factors.

6. Tabulations of environments permitting Rʔ and ʔR in Samish show
that: /R'/-> syllabic R̩ʔ /#C_#, CC_v´, C_C(C)VCV´, v´CC(C)_(C)(CV)#
          -> R' very rarely /V´_V, V´_C(C)#, V_V´
          -> Rʔ /elsewhere _C, V_V´, _#
          -> ʔR preferentially, but also Rʔ /V´_V

‑› R occasionally in the speech of VU and TB (less in that of LD)
This is a rule of allophony for all Samish glottalized resonants. There
is also a morphophonemic rule at a higher level which operates after
all affixing is done; it converts //ʔ-R// and //R-ʔ// both to /R'/.
There is also an optional later morphophonemic rule partially dependent
on the speed of speech, which allows deletion of /ə/ and feeds into the
rules producing syllabic resonants (both glottalized and plain).
Examples of the allophonic rule of decomposition of glottalized resonants
include:

[ʔn̩ʔ#sɬíqʷ] 'your flesh'
[níɬ#kʷn̩ʔ#ténhelə?] 'that's you folks' mother'
LD [sčn̩ʔéwxʷ], VU [sčən̩ʔéwtxʷ] 'pit-house, potato house, potato pit'
VU [č̓m̩ʔčəyí] 'ant'
LD [kʷm̩ʔstəlíʔqʷ ~ kʷumʔstəlíʔqʷ] 'mushroom'
VU [pítšn̩ʔ] 'lizard'
[q̓ə́mqsn̩ʔ] 'automobile'
LD [θ̓əlʔθ̓sástn̩ʔɬ], VU [θ̓əlʔθ̓sástn̩ʔɬtə] 'he hit us all in the face'
 (literally a passive: 'we were hit in the face')
 (rare instance of VU using [θ̓]; also note VU -ɬtə = LD -ɬ)
For examples of phonetic R' see above under paragraph 3.
[sə́lʔsəlʔtn̩] 'old-fashioned wool-spinner'
[stəšélʔqən?] 'a wool-carder'
[ɬəlʔtást] 'splashing him'
LD [skʷəlʔkʷə́θ̓], VU [skʷəlʔkʷə́c̓] 'real crooked'
[šq̓ayʔénʔč] 'rudder of boat'
[q̓xʷówʔɬ] 'second biggest canoe' (prob. loan ‹ Halkomelem)
LD [hiʔθ̓ɬánʔst] 'fall (season)'
LD [siyámʔst], VU [siyʔámʔsət] 'getting rich'
[q̓p̓éˆlʔssn̩?] 'I'm patching it' ([s·] would be more characteristic)
[xʷə́yʔtsən] 'I'm waking him up'
[sqə́mʔqsən] 'he has a sharp nose'
LD [p̓əlʔp̓ɬíkʷs] ~ VU, LD [p̓əlʔp̓əɬə́č̓ɬ] 'a lot hatched'
VU [táq̓ʷn̩ʔsən] 'I'm coughing'
LD [čə́ləwʔst], VU [čə́ləwʔsət] 'turn oneself over'
[syə́nyənʔxʷ] 'black bass' ~ [syə́nʔyənʔxʷ] 'black rockfish'
VU [čxáləwʔsa?], LD [čxáʔləwʔs(ə)] 'splitting wood'
[xʷc̓sástən̩ʔsn̩] 'he hit me in the face (lit. I was hit in the face)'
 (rare example of an LD [c̓])
[ʔəlʔxəwʔé] 'pit-lamping (hunting or fishing by torchlight at night)'
[šəšpəlʔás] 'he's whistling'
[sčəwʔét] 'he knows it'
VU [c̓əmʔén?], LD [θ̓əmʔén?] 'arrow'
[kʷšéʔmən?] 'nickname'
[ʔéʔləŋənəkʷ] 'village'
[sɬáʔŋət] 'herring'

[səmáʔnəʔ] 'halibut hook'
LD [šƛpíʔwənʔ], VU [šƛpíwənʔ] 'shirt'
LD [shíˇʔyɪlʔəkʷ], VU [shéˆʔɪləkʷ] 'happy, proud'
[čə́mʔəš̌] 'herring eggs (just eaten raw)'
[ƛ̓ʷə́lʔə] 'belly'
VU [čálʔəqʷ] ~ [čáʔləqʷ] 'way up or back on land (away from the water)'
VU [šsəłqʷíŋʔəł], LD [səłqʷíŋʔəł] 'awl'
[stɪtíqíwʔalʔł] 'colt'
[sxʷáyʔɪł] 'awake'
[łək̓ʷšə́nʔətəŋ] 'they tripped him (lit. he was tripped)'

   These rules can't be confirmed in all respects for the speech of TB
because there is less available and because my transcriptions of the text
and citation forms show far fewer glottalized resonants in his speech.
There is one example showing a glottalized resonant reduplicated as a unit:
TB [sæ̓yʔsiyʔ] 'to fear, be afraid of' (VU, LD [sé̓yʔsiyʔ]). There is
also one example of syllabic glottalized resonant in a text:
TB [šák̓ʷŋ̓ʔ] 'bathe' or 'bathing'. TB retains glottalization of
resonants in final position more often than not: TB [čə́leyʔ] 'bark
(of plant)', [θíθ̇ə̇θ̇əmʔ] 'bird', [q̓ʷə́lənʔ] 'ear', [líʔɛlʔ ~ lé̓ʔɛlʔ]
'far', [k̓ʷə́ləwʔ] 'skin', [čéˆsənʔ] 'growing up', vs. [sqʷəméy] 'dog'
(VU [sqʷəméyʔ]), [sθ̇ámʔ] 'bone' (LD [sθ̇ámʔ], VU [scámʔ]), and [qə́lən]
'eye' (VU, LD [qə́lənʔ]). None of the speakers have initial R'.

   In medial positions TB retains enough glottalized resonants to show
similar patterns to VU and LD. Thus ʔR seems to be found only V´_V
while Rʔ is also found there and elsewhere.
TB [síʔmatŋ ~ símatŋ] 'freeze', [ləlǽʔnŋ] 'hear', [stáʔləwʔ] 'river',
   [məmíʔmən] 'small, little' (VU, LD [ʔəmíʔmənʔ]); [θ̇íŋʔəl] 'near,
   close by', [čečéyʔɛƛ] 'short' (LD [čɪčáyʔɪƛ], VU [čečáyɛƛ]).
TB [sʔəlʔǽluxʷ] 'old people' (VU [sʔəlʔéluxʷ]), [xʷənʔéŋ] 'kind of,
   same as' (VU [xʷənʔéŋ ~ xʷənʔéŋ]̓), [nəθ̇ǽ·lʔŋuxʷ] 'different peoples,
   different tribes', [kʷikʷənʔtíŋʔələsən] 'I was held by someone',
   [ʔəwʔ#k̓ʷínʔalʔ] (# may be absent) 'few', [sčiyʔáłələ] 'used to get
   wood'.
Some examples of TB's medial loss of glottalized resonants (or VU/LD's
   addition of them) include: TB [ʔənǽ] (VU [ʔənʔé]) 'come', [tsál·lŋuxʷ]
   (VU [tsálʔŋuxʷ]) 'animal', [swéyəqə] (VU [swéyʔəqaʔ], LD [swéyʔqaʔ])
   'man, male', [x̌ə́wəs] (VU [x̌ə́wʔəs]) 'new'; this seems part of a process
   of TB's loss of /ʔ/ adjacent to other consonants: TB [ʔáyæθ] (VU, LD
   [ʔáyaʔs] 'have a sharp edge', [x̌ʷíx̌ʷɔx̌ʷi] (VU [x̌ʷíx̌ʷɔʔx̌ʷiyʔ], LD
   [x̌ʷíʔx̌ʷɔʔx̌ʷiyʔ]) 'narrow', [hǽ·łtən] (VU [hǽʔłtŋ]) 'they (these
   people)' (gloss approximate from text).

1.1.4. Vowels

1.1.4.1. /i/

Samish /i/ has allophones [i], [ɪ], [iˇ], [eˆ], and perhaps [əy] (if the latter isn't a morphophonemic variant, /əy/). [ɪ] is front lower high and lax and occurs stressed before /ŋ/ and /ŋ̇/, and unstressed in the following positions: before palatals /č,č̓,š/ (especially when /i/ also follows palatals or alveolars), and after palatals /y,ẏ,č,č̓,š/ especially when /i/ also precedes palatals, alveolars, or /m,m̓/).

_ŋ: θ̇,t,n,c̓,s,ł,č,k̓ʷ,q,ŋ,qʷ,q̓ʷ,ʔ_
_č: t,n,ł̓,č,š,y,xʷ,w̓,ʔ_
_č̓: l,š,ʔ_
_š: l,ł̓,k̓ʷ_
y,ẏ_m,m̓
y_m,t,(θ,g̱),s,k̓,ł,ł̓,č,ʔ
č_n,s,ł̓,č,ŋ
š_l,č

   Thus for example:
LD [łθ̇íŋən] '(a) comb' (VU [łc̓íŋən])
VU [štíŋət] 'wish for it'
LD [pək̓ʷìŋəłéwxʷ] 'smoking shed'
[səqíŋəł#sqéws] 'baked potatoes (baked in oven)'
LD [səłqʷíŋʔəł], VU [šsəłqʷíŋʔəł] 'awl'
TB [θ̇íŋʔəl] 'near, close by'
VU [słɛnɪčá·ł] 'young girl'
[t̓əmóʔlɪč] ~ [t̓əmúʔləč] 'barrel, tub'
[šɪčqʷí·læʔ] 'brushing [for spiritual cleansing, with cedar boughs]
 (a longhouse, a person, a home [in which a death has happened])'
[yíčət] 'bow (the weapon)' (it seems the palatal environment is
 sometimes strong enough to trigger [ɪ] even under stress)
[šqé·lɪč̓] 'modern wool-spinner'
VU [šéšɪč̓] 'woods'
VU [sk̓ʷəlʔíš] 'gun'
LD [šɪlɪšk̓ʷám̓ʔ], VU [šɪlɪšk̓ʷém̓ʔ] 'many swimming'
TB [q̓ʷəyí·lɪš] 'to dance'
[sk̓ʷíš] 'name'
[sk̓ʷáyɪmaʔ] (LD aʔ ~ əʔ) 'underbrush'
VU [sx̱ʷíyʔɪmʔ], LD [sx̱ʷíyʔím̓ʔ] 'story (legend) from way back, rock
 with spirit in it'
[t̓áyɪmʔt] 'put it on (of any clothing, shoes, pants, hat, etc.)'
TB [smáyɪθ], VU [smáyɪθ] (θ ~ g̱ ~ s), LD [smáyɪs] 'deer, (deer) meat'
[šéyɪł] 'older sibling, cousin through older sibling'

VU [yí?yɪ?xəm?], LD [yí?yxəm?] 'black huckleberry'
[ləščɪnánət] 'poor'
[sqʷəqʷem?éy?čɪs] 'pussy willow (lit. "puppy in the hand")
TB [ɬq̓ǽčɪs], VU [ɬq̓éčɪs] 'five'
TB [skʷǽčɪl], VU [skʷéčɪl] 'day'

    I should mention here that it is not always easy to distinguish [ɪ]
from [ɨ], the raised and fronted allophone of /ə/, which sometimes
occurs in similar environments. (Historically Straits and Halkomelem
have both changed many cases of unstressed /i/ to /ə/, thus causing
some of this complication.) Some of these cases can be seen when the
same morphemes appear affixed under different stress patterns. A
few can be seen when speakers differ, one using [ɪ] and others using
[ɨ]. In some cases [ɪ] was transcribed where [ɨ] should have been
and vice versa.

    The allophone [iˇ] occurs word-finally under stress for VU where LD
seems to have [i]. VU's [iˇ] seems somewhat laxed as well as lowered.
It is sometimes in free variation with [ɪ]. Some examples include:
VU [hayí ~ hayíˇ], LD [hayí], TB [həyíˇ] 'big'
VU [qʷəníˇ], LD [qʷəní] 'seagull'
VU [səmíˇ?], LD [səmí?] 'blanket (any kind)' (here the effect occurs
 even with a final /?/)

    /i/ has a rare allophone [eˆ], tense raised upper mid front unrounded
vowel, (sometimes in variation with [iˇ]) when stressed and adjacent to
postvelar and glottal obstruents. Plain [i] also occurs here however
and seems to be more frequent in these positions. When following a
postvelar, stressed /i/ allophones are sometimes preceded by a schwa
on-glide; when followed by a postvelar, they are sometimes followed
by a schwa off-glide. Since the phoneme /e/ has allophones including
[e] and [eˇ] (among others), the [eˆ] allophone of /i/ is occasionally
hard to distinguish; the allophones of /e/ however do not seem to have
schwa glides adjacent to postvelars.

    Some examples of [eˆ] and [iˇ] include the following:
[nəq̓éˆx] 'black'
VU [x̣éˆɬət] 'scratch it (on purpose)'
VU [steqéw ~ stiᵊqéw] 'horse' (Halkomelem [stiᵊqíw])
[səqíˇws ~ səqéˆws] 'pants'
[čx̣íˇqʷt#tə#sq̓wáŋi?] 'split (a) fish head'
LD [čqʷíˇl?s] 'person who does burnings for the dead'
[tqíˇp ~ tqéˆp] 'big fish trap (round, used in ocean)'
LD [heˆyəqsn̩], VU [híˇyəqsn̩] 'have a wide nose'
Examples are few compared to other Straits dialects. The norms for both

/i/and /e/ seem to be higher for Samish than for Lummi for example.

[əy] seems to occur in both stressed and unstressed positions as an
alternate to [i] in careful pronunciation and often after postvelars.
[əy] in the latter environment probably reflects the schwa on-glide and
a lowered allophone of /i/. For example:
VU [ləŋə́yt ~ ləŋít], LD [ləŋít] 'watching it, looking at it'
VU [swə́y?qɛ? ~ swéy?qɛ?], LD [swíy?qə?] 'man' (VU's [ɛ] also reflects
 a slower more careful pronunciation)
[slə́wəy? ~ slə́wiy?] 'cedar bark'
[čə́ləy? ~ čə́li?] 'bark of fir or balsam'
LD [x̣əy?ə́m?nəč], VU [x̣eyə́m?nəč] 'tree trunk and roots, stump' (LD's
 retention of [y?] is evidence of slower/more careful pronunciation in
 contrast to VU's [y])
[sx̣ə́yx̣əyƛ̓] 'cod eggs (picked up and eaten raw if fresh)' (could also
 show /əy/ in both places)

Elsewhere /i/ has allophone [i] (optionally with schwa on-glides
after postvelars and schwa off-glides before postvelars, as mentioned).
No examples of both on-glides and off-glides on the same allophone have
been found so far; where postvelars surround /i/, the schwa off-glide
seems to be retained while the on-glide is dropped.

Some examples of [i] include:
[šx̣ʷsílə?] 'grandparent-in-law'
[sⱡíⱡiy?] 'ashamed to take a slave'
[ƛ̓íƛ̓etəl] 'loving each other'
[?i], TB [?i] (normal speed, text) ~ [?é·] (slow citation) 'and'
[p̓íp̓kʷtən] 'a float'
[p̓íkʷən] 'split roasting-stick'
[sx̣ʷiy?ém?] 'story'
VU [qʷíˀx̣ʷət], LD [qʷíx̣ʷt] 'miss it; move it'
[sx̣ʷíx̣ʷq̓ʷⱡnəⱡ] 'anything around the neck (cloth, neckerchief, necklace)'
VU [ċístən] 'horn, antler'
VU [x̣čítsən] 'I know him'
[stíšəm] 'fish slime'
[si?ít] 'true, truly'
Examples of unstressed [i] are quite rare except before y(?)# (where they
 could also be heard as [ə] /ə/). This is the result of a historical
 change shared within Straits and Halkomelem (see above).

1.1.4.2. /e/
    Samish front unrounded /e/ has allophones [e] (upper-mid tense),
[eˇ] (lowered upper-mid to mean-mid tense), [ɛˆ] (raised lower-mid to
mean-mid tense), [ɛ] (lower-mid lax), [ɛˇ] (lowered lower-mid tense),

and [æ] (upper-low lax). The distribution and frequency of these are
similar for LD and VU but rather different for TB. For LD and VU
[e] and [eˇ] are the most frequent (55.2 percent of the words with /e/
had these), [εˆ], [ε], and [εˇ] are the next most frequent (34.3 percent),
and [æ] is the least frequent (10.5 percent). For TB [æ] is the most
frequent (78.5 percent), [ε] is next most frequent (12.3 percent), and
[e] is least frequent (9.2 percent, 6 examples which either vary with /i/
[i], appear as [i] or [eˆ] for the other speakers, or could be transcribed
as [əy] /i/). (None of these counts includes texts.)

For TB, [ε] is rare in citations (8 examples) and is never cited under
stress. It is more frequent in the text but still not as frequent as [æ];
in the text [ε] appears stressed a few times (mainly before /ŋ/ or /ŋ̇/
as with LD and VU), but in both the text and the citations [ε] is
clearly the unstressed allophone of /e/. [æ] on the other hand is
almost always stressed (42 out of 51 citations); half of the cases of
unstressed [æ] are echo vowels in the environment ǽʔ_. In the text of
TB [æ] only appears stressed or in the position of an echo vowel, i.e.
in the environment ǽʔ_. In the text [e] only appears a few times
and always as a stressed allophone of /i/.
For TB then, /e/ has allophones:
[æ] under stress (except _ŋ,ŋ̇) and ǽʔ_
[ε] elsewhere (stressed _ŋ,ŋ̇, and unstressed)
([e] is an allophone of /i/).

For LD and VU the situation is reversed in some respects. All the
allophones of /e/ appear stressed most of the time in citations.
[e] and [eˇ] are unstressed in only 34 out of 407 words (8.35 percent),
[εˆ], [ε], and [εˇ] are unstressed in 65 out of 253 words (25.7 percent),
and [æ] is unstressed in 15 out of 77 words (19.5 percent).

The 34 examples of unstressed [e] and [eˇ] occur in the following conditions: five vary with [i] or are errors for [eˆ] (allophones of /i/),
fourteen are echoes in the phonemic environment éʔ_,
ten occur in the environment _y,ẏ where they are likely [ə] /ə/,
and the remainder appear to be errors for varieties of [ε].

The 15 examples of unstressed [æ] occur as follows: five occur as
echoes in the environment éʔ_ (ǽʔæ), six vary with [ε], and four
vary with [ə].

The 65 examples of unstressed [εˆ], [ε], and [εˇ] occur as follows:
14 are echoes in the environment of éʔ_ (mostly έʔε, έˇʔεˇ, and έˆʔεˆ),
18 or more occur C_(ʔ)# (where C = consonant, usually a palatal),
some vary with [ə] and may reflect a fronted allophone of /ə/ adjacent

to palatal consonants (perhaps something like [ə ͨ]), the rest seem
to be the unstressed allophone of /e/ for LD and VU, as well as for TB.

A word should be said about the phonemic environment é?_ which
conditions unstressed /e/ allophones for LD, VU, and TB. In most
cases the unstressed allophone matches the stressed one. In some cases
the unstressed allophone is shifted to a more mid allophone. Compare
the following:
VU [pé?ekʷ] 'pipe (for stove or tobacco)'
VU [spé?es ~ spéˇ?ɛˆs], LD [spéˆ?ɛˆθ ~ spéˇ?ɛˆθ] 'bear'
VU [qʷǽ?en], LD [qʷé?en ~ qʷé?n] 'mosquito'
[qé?exʷ] 'crabapple'
LD [sχéˆ?ɛˆs], VU [sχéˇ?ɛˇs], TB [χǽ?æs] 'bad'
VU [hǽ:?æ] 'yes'

An interesting fact to notice is that LD often uses the highest
allophones, VU the next highest, and TB the lowest allophones of /e/.
This can be seen in the word for 'bad' just above and in a number of
other examples such as:
LD [šxʷ?iléwa?], VU [šxʷ?iléwə?] 'turnip' (loan < Chinook Jargon)
LD [ləhéˇl?], VU [ləhéˆl?] 'the bone game, slahal game'
LD [ləhéˇ?ɛˆl?], VU [ləhéˆ?ɛl?] 'playing slahal'
LD [χéˇ?eˇl?s], VU [χéˇ?ɛl?s] 'the Transformer'
LD [péˇeyčən], VU [pǽ(?)eyčən] 'fishing rod; fishing boat'
LD [stéˇləŋuxʷ ~ stéləŋuxʷ], VU [stéˇlŋuxʷ ~ stéˇlŋuxʷ] 'medicine'
LD [?əséˆqɬ], VU [?əséqɬ] 'outside'
TB [nə́ċɛ#snǽčəwəč], VU [nə́ċɛ#snéˇčəwəč], LD [nə́ċə#néčəwəč] 'one
 hundred'
TB [stǽskʷəɬ], VU [stéˆskʷəɬ], LD [stéˆskʷɬ] 'back'
TB [mǽn], LD, VU [méˆn] 'father'
TB [ƛ̇ǽqæ?], VU, LD [ƛ̇éˇqə?] 'liver'

When the allophones of /e/ are charted on a grid of adjacent consonants
for VU and LD the following patterns show up:
[e] can occur in any of the environments
[eˇ], [ɛˆ], [ɛ], [ɛˇ], and [æ] occur _R,R',Q,? (Q = postvelars, R' =
 glottalized resonants, R = plain resonant); in these environments they
 vary freely with each other and with [e] (but some preferences have been
 noted above)
[æ] is found more often adjacent to Q or before ?
[æ] can acquire a [y] off-glide Q_N,N' (N = nasal, N' = glottalized nasal)
[æ] sometimes acquires a [y] on-glide ŋ_Q

Examples of these rules are plentiful above except for the two about glides:
[qǽyʔŋi?] 'teenaged girl'

VU [sƛ̓q̓ǽyn? ~ sƛ̓q̓έ˄?εn], LD [sƛ̓q̓é?εn] 'long feather'
VU [ŋyǽqə? ~ ŋyéqə? ~ ŋéqə?], LD [ŋyéqə? ~ ŋéqə?], TB [ŋǽqæ?]
'fallen snow'

1.1.4.3. /ə/

/ə/ has the following allophones for all three speakers:
[ʌ] under stress (transcribed as [ə́])
[ə ~ ɨ] unstressed and adjacent to palatals or _N,N'
[ʊ] unstressed and adjacent to labialized obstruents (rarely ~ [ə])
perhaps also unstressed and adjacent to bilabials (often ~ [ə])
[ə] elsewhere

For example:
[sə́ni?] 'short Oregon grape berry'
[t̓ə́qʷʊm?] 'thimbleberry'
[pqʷə́čən], TB [pqʷə́čn̩] 'sand'
VU [ƛ̓šə́nəp] 'plow'
VU [ləq̓ə́s̩ət] 'line it up, make yourself even (of people, canoes, etc.)'
TB, VU, LD [t̓x̣ə́ŋ] 'six'
LD [tə́kʷxʷ], TB, VU [tə́kʷʊxʷ] 'nine'
TB, LD [nə́θ̓ə], VU [nə́c̓a? ~ nə́c̓ə] 'one'
LD, TB [čə́sæ?], VU [čə́sa? ~ čə́sə?] 'two'
VU [x̣ə́yəmnɨč] ~ LD, VU [x̣əy?ə́mnəč] 'snag, stump'
LD [swí?wəlɨs ~ swí?wələs], VU [swí?wələs] 'teenaged boy'
VU [čɨlčə́qʷ] 'on fire, be burning'
[stámɨš] 'warrior'
TB [ɬq̓ǽčɨs], VU [ɬq̓ečɨs ~ ɬq̓ə́yčɨs], LD [ɬq̓é(y)čs] 'five'
[x̣ə́yčŋ̩ ~ x̣éčŋ̩], TB [x̣ǽčɨŋ] 'dry'
VU [?ɨn?é ~ ?ən?έ], TB [?ɨnǽ ~ ?ənǽ] 'come'
[syə́wɨn] 'spirit song and dance'
VU [tsál?ŋʊxʷ], TB [tsá·lŋʊxʷ] 'animal'
[č̓á?muqʷ] 'great grandparent; great grandchild'
VU [núkʷ ~ nə́kʷ], LD [nə́kʷ] '(it's) you (sg.)'
[sx̣ə́p̓ʊk̓ʷ] 'soft edible bone in fish head'
VU [k̓ʷʊl?k̓ʷəl?έ˅x̣ən?] 'butterfly'
VU [xʷʊnítm̩] 'white man'
[sɬék̓ʷʊŋ] 'breath (noun)'
VU [?əw?#léŋənʊxʷsənsə?] 'I'll see you'

There are a few cases of unstressed [ʊ ~ ə] adjacent to bilabials;
[ə] is much more common in this position.
[nupə́t ~ nəpə́t] 'to advise someone'
VU [šéšʊm?] 'shallow'
LD [šqətéw?ʊɬ] 'bridge'

[sčí?wup̓] 'tight (clothes, in box)'
[wuwəsél?s ~ wəwəsél?s] 'he's barking (of a dog)'

1.1.4.4. /u/

/u/ is a rare phoneme, appearing mainly in loanwords from Chinook Jargon,
European and other Amerindian languages. (A sound shift affecting Halkomelem and dialects of Northern Straits [Saanich, Songish, and Samish]
changed */u/ to /ə/.) The examples of Samish [u] which are not in
apparent loans appear to be cases of /ə/ → [u] before bilabial /w,w̓/
in unstressed positions or of schwa deletion and vocalization of //w,w̓//
to /u,u?/. These cases often vary with [əw] and can be shown to
consist of //əw//, morphophonemically. There are also a few cases
of this which occur under stress.

/u/ in spite of all that does appear to have some allophones. A few
cases of [ŭ] or [u^] occur word-finally (sometimes other speakers have
[u] in those places). Also a few cases of genuine [o] occur in some
loans (sometimes in free variation with [u]). Otherwise [u] is the
expected allophone.

   Examples of /u/ include:
[k̓wúyukw] 'fish hook' (probable loan)
VU [pútəlkwəs], LD [pútəl?kwəs] 'oar' (root is loan < English "boat")
VU [pút] 'boat'
VU [yé?#kwə#skwúl] 'go to school'
[skwúkwəl] 'he's/she's in school' (root < English with Samish reduplication)
VU [kwú·l] 'gold' (prob. < Chinook Jargon < English)
VU [kəpú], LD [kəpú^] 'coat' (< Chinook Jargon < French "capote")
[həm?ú] 'pigeon' (widely disseminated throughout Northwest in unrelated
  languages, see Seaburg 1985)
[músməs] 'cow' (< Chinook Jargon)
[q̓xʷów?ł] 'second biggest canoe' (prob. < Halkomelem where it has just
  this form)
[swóq̓wəł] 'goat wool blanket' (prob. < Halkomelem where it has just this
  form and whose people had access to mountain goat unlike the Straits
  people)
[t̓əmó?lɨč ~ t̓əmú?ləč] 'barrel, tub'

   Examples of /əw/ [uw ~ əw] include:
particle /?əw̓/ 'contrastive   (often with contrast to an earlier
  clause or sentence)' (precedes verb, often suffixed to other preposed
  particles, works much as in Saanich, see Montler 1985:194–197):
  VU [?uw? x̣čítsən kwsə q̓æy?ŋi?] 'I know the girl.'
  VU [?əw? x̣čítɬtə kwsə q̓æy?ŋi?] 'We know the girl.'

VU [láʔa kʷoʔ lǽʔæ] 'it's over there' (//kʷ-ʔəẃ//)

VU [siʔítuʔ nás] 'extremely fat' (//siʔít-ʔəẃ//)

[suʔ] 'so, then' (//s-ʔəẃ//)

LD [luwʔ] 'past　　contrastive　　' (//l-ʔəẃ//)

VU [sčəqʷóʔsəʔ ~ sčəqʷəẃʔsə], LD [sčə́qʷəẃ(sə)] 'fire'

[ƛúƛaʔ] 'small' vs. VU [ƛəƛə́ẃƛaʔ] 'a few small ones'

LD [sčuwʔét] 'smart, know how to'

TB [túlə ~ túlə nə́θ̓ɛ] 'an other'

(In these examples I have replaced [#] with a space to show words more clearly.)

1.1.4.5. /a/

Samish /a/ has two allophones, [ɔ] and [a]. [ɔ] is rather rare
compared to [a]; for example I count only 26 examples of [ɔ] in all
the citations but 110 examples of unstressed [a] alone and many more
of stressed [a].

ɔ́:
q̇ʷ_ŋ ~a
n_qʷ ~a
t_qʷ ~a
qʷ_qʷ
q̇ʷ_q̇
q̇ʷ_m
m_ŋ ~a
n_ŋ ~a
qʷ_ʔw
qʷ_ʔt ~a
qʷ_m ~a
q̇ʷ_q̇ʷ
w_q̇ʷ
k̇ʷ_qʷ
kʷ_m
š_l < Chinook Jargon
m_qʷ
qʷ_qʷ
q̇ʷ_q̇ʷ ~a

ɔ: x̣ʷ_ʔx̣ʷ, x̣ʷ_x̣ʷ TB, qʷ_qʷ, q̇ʷ_q

From the above environments it is quite clear that [ɔ] occurs
(often in free variation with [a]) flanked by a labialized postvelar
on one side and a (labialized) postvelar, labialized velar, or a labial
resonant on the other side. Only rarely is one of the postvelars not
labialized (ŋ,q,q̇); those cases all have [a] as the more frequent
variant allophone. Four cases occur of an alveolar consonant flanking
and again they have [a] as the more frequent variant allophone. One
other case occurs of [ɔ] in an environment other than those mentioned
but it is VU, LD [ləšɔ́l] 'shawl', clearly a borrowing from Chinook
Jargon leshawl 'shawl'. An interesting pair is VU's citation of
[sɔ́ŋ] as Lummi and [sáŋ] as Samish for 'go up (a hill)'; the Lummi
norm for /a/ is [ɔ] (Charles, Demers and Bowman 1978).

Unstressed [ɔ] is even more rare. In fact most of the examples go
back to //ə// morphophonemically. They may be slightly rounded and
lowered allophones of /ə/, mistranscribed as [ɔ], or they may be

genuine unstressed [ɔ], found in the predicted environments but
proportionately more rare than stressed [ɔ]. If they are the latter
a morphophonemic rule would be required for them, //ə// -> /a/,
or morphophonemically a new reduplication type would have to be
posited for them.

Unstressed [a] in the environment _(ʔ)# appears only in careful
pronunciation. In normal or allegro speech it changes to [ə].

Some examples of /a/ include the following:
[sq̇ʷóq̇ʷiyʔ] ~ [sq̇ʷáq̇ʷəyʔ] 'dead'
[č̵lqʷómə? ~ č̵lqʷámə?] 'blackcap berry'
VU [qʷóqʷɔcqʷə?], TB [qʷá?qʷə] 'to drink'
[šq̇ʷóq̇ʷɔqsn] 'the whole world' (//-əqsən// 'point, nose')
VU [wóq̇ʷəł], LD [wóq̇ʷł] 'downstream'
VU [c̀əmóŋəsətsən ~ θ̇əmóŋəsətsən] 'I'm getting wet', VU [c̀əmáŋəgət]
 ~ [c̀əmáŋəθət] 'to get wet'
VU [səłqʷ́ɔ?wəč] 'to get a hole in it'
[sq̇ʷóŋi? ~ sq̇ʷáŋi?] 'head'
[qʷɔqʷí(yɪ)łč] 'arbutus tree'
VU [x̣ʷíx̣ʷɔ?x̣ʷiyʔ], LD [x̣ʷí?x̣ʷɔ?x̣ʷiyʔ] 'thin (for ex. tree or rope)',
 TB [x̣ʷíᵍx̣ʷɔx̣ʷi] 'narrow'
[qəlí:ma?] 'dirty (of physical or verbal qualities)' but
 VU [qəlí:mə? (?)éˇ?lən?] 'dirty house'
[?éˆła?] 'here' but VU [?éˆłə? tə sqʷəméy?] 'the dog is here'
[s?áłqa? ~ s?áłqə?] 'snake'
[x̣ʷux̣ʷtəm?iyáč] 'grasshopper'
[qətqətčálə?] 'spider'
[pápəqʷ] 'mouldy'
[sk̇ʷtá?] 'raven'
[swákʷən] 'loon'

1.1.5. Length and Stress

/·/ has two allophones, [:] and [·]. The former occurs only after
stressed vowels in a few examples in careful speech and as emphatic length
(sometimes even [:·]) in stories and conversations. The latter, [·],
occurs after spirants and non-glottalized resonants; a morphophonemic
rule, mentioned in the discussion of consonant allophony above, changes
geminate spirants and resonants to spirant/resonant plus length (see 1.1.1
for examples). [·] also occurs after stressed vowels occasionally, for
example:
[číˑyɛ?] 'bluejay'
VU [q̇ayéˆˑč] 'elk'
TB [q̇ʷəyíˑłɛ̌], VU, LD [q̇ʷəyíləš] 'dance'

[sčé·nuxʷ], TB [sčǽ·nuxʷ] 'fish'
VU [sqé·mukʷ ~ sqémukʷ] '(small) octopus'
VU [(s)qəm?k̓ʷá·ɫ] 'big octopus"
VU [hǽˆ:?æ] 'yes'
VU [k̓ʷú·l] 'gold' (< Chinook Jargon)
TB [tsá·lŋυxʷ], VU [tsál?ŋυxʷ] 'animal'
TB [sŋǽ·nt], VU [sŋé·nt] 'rock, mountain'
There are no attestations of length (other than emphatic) after /ə/.

Stress has not been found to be predictable and thus is phonemic.
There are subminimal pairs (see below). I have occasionally transcribed
secondary stress, [`], within a word, but so rarely that I believe it is
probably mistranscription. This seems confirmed by the fact that it is
not attested consistently from one citation of a given word to another.

1.2. SOME MINIMAL AND SUBMINIMAL PAIRS

Minimal pairs are a helpful shortcut to determine phonemic contrasts
and provide useful confirmation of such contrasts. They are no substitute
for tabulation of environments which provide the predictive power of
phonemic descriptions. Due to the large number of phonemes in Samish
there are fewer minimal pairs than in languages with a smaller phonemic
inventory. The fact that Samish is more synthetic than analytic also
diminishes the chances of minimal pairs. However by eliciting data
cognate with minimal pairs in other Straits dialects and in Halkomelem
it has been possible to find some sets sooner than by accident.
Here are a few minimal and subminimal pairs found in Samish to date.
More of these are from VU because there was little need to re-elicit
them from LD.

[səw?níɫ] 'him' vs. VU [cəw?níɫ], LD [θəw?níɫ] 'her'
[sə] 'the (female)' vs. [cə] 'the (male)' vs. [tə] 'the (visible, generally
 existent)' vs. [k̓ʷə] 'the (invisible, remote); [subordinator]' vs. [?ə]
 'oblique case marker (nominal phrase not co-referenced by verb affix)'
 vs. [nə] 'my'
[q̓ʷəyíləš] 'dance' vs. LD [q̓ʷəy?íləš], VU [q̓ʷəyíl?əš] 'dancing'
LD [qʷéləst] 'bail oneself' vs. LD, VU [qʷél?əst] 'boil something'
 vs. VU [k̓ʷél?əst] 'spill, overturn, capsize'
VU [tə́s] 'approach, get near' vs. VU [ɫə́s] 'it got smashed'
VU [qə́m?əl] 'tide starts to come in' vs. VU [qé·məl?] 'tide is coming
 right in'
VU [čáq̓ʷən] 'to sweat' vs. VU [čáx̣ʷən] 'to melt' vs. VU [čáq̓ʷəɫ]
 'it's burned' vs. VU [čə́q̓ʷ] 'get burned' vs. VU [čə́q̓] 'surprised'
 vs. LD [θ́áq̓ʷŋ̣(?)], VU [ċáq̓ʷŋ̣] 'rotten (of wood)'
VU [qʷé·l] 'talk' vs. VU [kʷé·l] 'to hide' vs. VU [q̓él?] 'believe' vs.

VU [kʷə́lʔ] 'spilled (of a container)' vs. VU [q̓ʷə́lʔ] 'ripe; cooked'
vs. VU [kʷú·l] 'gold'

VU [séxʷsəxʷ] 'to be lazy by nature' vs. [sáʔsx̣ʷ] 'damp (in the
morning), dew'

VU [q̓ʷə́lənʔ] 'ear' vs. VU [q̓ʷə́lənʔ] 'he's barbecuing' vs. VU [qə́lənʔ]
'eye' vs. VU [kʷə́lən] 'to fly'

VU [stén̓] 'what is it?' vs. VU [štə́n̓] 'to walk' vs. VU [štín̓ət]
'wish for it'

VU [píxʷət] 'shake it and make it fall, brush something off' vs.
VU [páxʷət] 'blow it up (with mouth), blow it off' vs. VU [puxʷél̓ʔs]
'blowing (of the wind)' vs. VU [péxʷən] 'it's stale, boring'

VU [sé̌səwʔ] 'beach' vs. VU [sásən] 'mouth'

VU [mə́q̓ʷ] 'it burst (of a sore)', VU [mə́k̓ʷ] 'all' vs. VU [máʔaqʷ]
'duck' vs. VU [mɔ́qʷ] '[stout (of a tree)] (in text)' vs. VU [mə́q̓]
'satiated with food, full'

VU [c̓ə́s] 'got hit (by something in air, ground, or water)' vs. VU
[tsás] 'poor (in wealth, spirits, etc.)'

VU [ləkəlít] 'lock it up' vs. [qəlét ~ qəlʔé̂t] 'again'

[ƛ̓ə́q̓ʷ] 'get stuck (like clothes in chair, etc.)' vs. VU [ɬə́q̓ʷ] 'it
peeled off (bark for ex.), came off (of something stuck on)' vs.
VU [ƛ̓ə́k̓ʷ] 'it went out (of fire)'

VU [tə́q̓ʷ] 'get tight' vs. VU [tə́k̓ʷ] 'to break (of a stick)' vs.
LD [t̓ə́kʷt̓ək̓ʷ] 'mud is loose' vs. [tə́q̓ʷtəq̓ʷ] 'red snapper'

LD [t̓áqaʔ] 'get bruised' vs. [t̓éqæ̓ʔ] 'salal berry'

VU [q̓ə́čəqs], LD [q̓ə́čqs] 'coho salmon (one kind)' vs. [q̓ə́čiyʔ] 'moss'

VU [hésn̓] 'to sneeze' vs. VU [sx̣ʷésən̓], LD [sx̣ʷésəm] 'soapberries,
Indian ice cream'

VU [xʷəčə́sət], LD [xʷəčə́st] 'wake up' vs. VU [xʷəč̓ə́sət], LD [xʷəč̓ə́st]
'go through a narrow place (in mountains, in crowd)'

VU [xʷéyləmʔ] 'rope' vs. VU [x̣ə́ləmʔ] 'small black Chinese slipper
(has something like teeth on outside)(limpet shell)(eaten after cooking)'

VU [láʔa] '[past]' vs. VU [lá̌ʔæ ~ lé̌ʔɛ ~ lěʔěʔ] 'there' vs. LD [lúʔu]
'[past contrastive]'

VU [háy] 'to finish' vs. VU [ʔə́yʔ] 'to be good'

[nás] 'to be fat' vs. [n̓ás] 'four'

[č̓x̣ə́t] 'tear it' vs. [č̓ə́x̣t] 'tearing it'

[ƛ̓pə́x̣t] 'scatter it' vs. [ƛ̓ə́pxt] 'scattering it'

[sx̣ə́t] 'push it' vs. [sə́x̣t] 'pushing it'

[č̓tə́n̓] 'crawl' vs. [č̓ə́tn̓ʔ] 'crawling'

2. MORPHOPHONEMICS (A BRIEF OUTLINE)

Several morphophonemic rules have already been referred to above:

1. A spirant or resonant -> /·/ after an identical spirant or resonant (1.1.1, 1.1.2, 1.1.5).

2. /?/ is inserted adjacent to resonants in the 'continuative aspect' (also known as the 'actual aspect' in the literature on Straits) (1.1.3).

3. /?R/ and /R?/ -> /R'/ (where R = resonant, R' = glottalized resonant) (1.1.3).

4. /m/ ~ /ŋ/ in some roots (1.1.3). The other Salish languages show /m/ for these forms and for all other cases of Straits /ŋ/ (except Twana and Lushootseed which show /b/ and other languages show traces an arrested sound change toward /b/ [for example, Comox and several old idiolects of Upriver Halkomelem, see Galloway 1982 and Thompson and Kinkade forthcoming]). I believe all these derive from a Proto-Central Salish */m/ (Kuipers 1970 and 1982, Galloway 1982) (Thompson 1979 proposes */ŋʷ/ for Proto-Salish and by implication for Proto-Central Salish).

5. /kʷ/ ~ /w/ (and /ẃ/) in some roots (1.1.3). Closely related is the rule that /č/ ~ /y/ [and /ẏ/] in some roots; cognates in most other Salish languages show that historically these alternations were produced by a sound change as follows: *y,*w -> Straits č,kʷ respectively, other languages y,w in the environment _V, *y,*w -> Straits (+ other Salish languages) y,w respectively elsewhere (i.e., _C,#). This rule however has not survived intact as a synchronic rule in Straits. There is now a more general tendency to use the resonant in the continuative aspect and the obstruent in the non-continuative, though traces of the original rule can also be seen.

6. Glottalized resonants are reduplicated as any other unit consonant is (1.1.3).

7. Samish has a number of types of reduplication, including at least C_1VC_2- 'plural' (where V = V_1 or /ə/), =$C_1əC_2$ 'characteristic' (where the equals sign shows the position of affixation of a derivational affix)(1.1.3), and others on pp.39, 45-47.

8. /ə/ is deleted optionally when unstressed in allegro speech; the rule is actually somewhat more complex than this I believe (1.1.3). For example, LD normally makes such a deletion in the environment C_C# (where C = any consonant) while VU and TB rarely make it except when the final consonant is a nasal. This rule feeds into the rule producing glottalized resonants (and so precedes it); it also feeds into the allophonic rule producing syllabic resonants.

9. (A phonotactic rule): Glottalized resonants are not attested word-initially (1.1.3).

10. /i/ may vary with /əy/ in some words (1.1.4.1).

11. There may be a morphophonemic rule inserting echo vowels between /ʔ/ and non-resonants in a number of words (1.1.4.2).

12. There is likely a rule vocalizing semivowels as follows: /y,ẏ,w,ẃ/ —› /i,iʔ,u,uʔ/ respectively in the environment C_ C,# (1.1.4.4).

13. /ʔəẃ/ —› /(ə)ẃ/ after most preverbal particles (1.1.4.4).

14. If unstressed [ɔ] is not mistranscribed for a slightly rounded and lowered allophone of /ə/ (which I believe it is), then either a morphophonemic rule /ə/ —› /a/ in certain unstressed environments is required or a new type of reduplication (C₁a-). Both seem unlikely (1.1.4.5).

15. Unstressed /a/ —› /ə/ in the environment _(ʔ)# (where the /ʔ/ is optional as shown by parentheses)(1.1.4.5).

Additional morphophonemic rules which must be present in Samish include:

16. Optional insertion of /ə/ in the environment R_ŋ,ŋ̇ (R = plain resonant). This rule is used much more frequently by LD than by VU; it is also attested in TB's speech.

17. Morphophonemic rules are required for specifying each distinct type of reduplication. Besides 'characteristic' and 'plural' reduplications Samish uses reduplications also for 'diminutive', 'continuative/actual aspect', and perhaps other aspects such as 'resultive' or 'durative' as well as some derivational processes.

18. Morphophonemic rules are required for several kinds of ablaut, metathesis, and stress shifting, all used in forming 'continuative aspect', 'plural', and some other aspects and derivations.

19. Morphophonemic rules are required for several infixes as well, for example //-əl- ~ -lə-// 'plural' and //-C₁V₁-// 'continuative aspect', to specify places of insertion and the lexically-determined and morphological classes to which they apply.

20. One or more morphophonemic rules are needed to describe the shifts of stress found when roots of different valences (strong = always retains stress, weak = never bears stress, neutral = bears stress in certain environments) are affixed with affixes with such stress valences. Most, if not all, combinations are attested in Samish.

Examples of the first fifteen rules except for 4, 5, and 12 can be found in the sections mentioned but a few more are given here. Examples of rules 15, 16, 17, 18, and 19 are also present in some of the forms given but are not easily found there; some examples are given here also, along with examples of rules 4, 5, 12, and 20. Some affixes may not be segmented yet. Hyphens separate inflectional affixes, equals separate derivational affixes; infixes are shown enclosed in square brackets and either hyphens or equals signs as appropriate. Morphophonemic transcrip-

tion is enclosed in double slashes; allomorphs can be seen within phonemic
single slashes but segmented with hyphens or equal signs.

1. //s-símaʔ// TB /s·íməʔ/ ([g·íməʔ]), VU /síməʔ/ 'ice'
VU //k̓ʷés=sət// /k̓ʷés·ət/ 'it's getting warmer [or get hot]'
VU //kʷən-nəxʷ nə s-c̓áɬ=əŋ// /kʷən·uxʷ nə sc̓áɬŋ/ 'I have a cold'

2.//kʷín-təl// 'to fight' vs. //kʷí[-w-ʔ-]ən[-ʔ-]-təl -ʔ //
/kʷíwəntəl̓/ [kʷíʔwənʔtəlʔ] 'fighting'
//ɬəlt=ás-t// 'splash him' vs. //ɬəl[-ʔ-]t=ás-t// /ɬəl̓tást/
[ɬəlʔtást] 'splashing him'
//čáwə=sət// LD /čák̓ʷəsət/, VU /čák̓ʷəsət/ 'to show off' vs.
//čáw[-ʔ-]=sət// LD, VU /čáw̓st/ [čáwʔst] 'showing off'

3. see the examples in 2 just above

4. /méq̓/ 'full (of stomach), satiated (with food)' vs. LD /ŋəq̓ə́-t/,
VU /ŋq̓ə́-t/ [ŋ̓q̓ə́t] 'swallow it'

5. //s=ɬénəy=ʔ// /sɬéniy̓/ 'lady, woman' vs. //s=ɬénəy=áɬ//
/sɬénəčá·ɬ/ 'girl (around 14)'
//wín=təl// /kʷíntəl/ 'they fought' vs. //wí[-Cˌə-]n-təl// +
'continuative' glottalization -> //wíw[-ʔ-]ən[-ʔ]təl[-ʔ]//
/kʷíwəntəl̓/ [kʷíʔwənʔtəlʔ] 'they're fighting' (shows that the
reduplication is infixed first, then the glottal stops after each
resonant (stopping the second w from becoming kʷ), then rule 5
is applied after all infixing; an alternate analysis would have the
root be //kʷín// 'grab' (cf. /kʷə́n-ət/ 'grab it', /kʷə́n-nəxʷ/
'hold it, take it') + //-təl// 'reciprocal' but requiring rule 5
to also work in the reverse, /kʷ/ -> /w/ before consonant or pause;
the second treatment seems to be historically accurate since the
root has /kʷ/ in all three words in non-Straits cognates)
//qíw-əŋ// /qík̓ʷəŋ/ [qéˆk̓ʷəŋ] 'rested' vs. //s-qí[-ʔ-qə-]w[-ʔ]//
/sqíʔqəw̓/ [sqíˇʔqəwʔ] 'be resting' (resultive/durative aspect)
//čáwə=s// /čák̓ʷs/ 'use it' vs. //čá[-ʔá-]w[-ʔ-]=s// /čaʔáw̓əs/
[čaʔáʔwəs] 'using it' (note that the non-continuative form probably
had a stage /čák̓ʷəs/ then deleted /ə/ due to rule 8; the continuative
on the other hand kept the /w/ due to insertion of /ʔ/, converted it to
/w̓/, then added an epenthetic /ə/; or the continuative followed the
pattern of resonant in continuative; aspect in Straits is often very
complex phonologically)
//séwə=s// VU /sék̓ʷəs/, LD /sék̓ʷs/ 'put it down' vs. //sé[-é-]w[-ʔ-]=s//
/seʔéw̓əs/ VU [seʔéʔwəs], LD [seʔéw̓ʔəs ~ seʔéw̓əs] 'putting it down'
//máy-t// /mác̓t/ 'aim it' vs. VU //s-má[-ʔ-ma-]y-t-əŋ// /smám̓aytŋ/,
LD //s-má[-ʔ-mə-]y-t-əŋ// /smám̓əytŋ/ 'it was aimed' (resultive

aspect, note different reduplication and /ʔ/-infix pattern)
//néy-ən// /néčəŋ/ 'to laugh' vs. //nə-néy-əŋ[-ʔ]// /nənéyəŋ/
'laughing' (note prefixed continuative reduplication for this root)

6. see all of the examples found so far, in 1.1.3, argument 2.

7. see examples in 5 and 6 above

8. A number of examples have been given in section 1; a few more are
'use it' and 'put it down' in 5 above, as well as:
VU /sléčəɫ/, LD /sléǝɫ/ 'it is full'
VU /sŋétxʷəns/, LD /sŋétxʷns/ 'mother's brother's wife'
VU /šípət/, LD /šípt/ 'sharpen it'
VU /ƛ́əpxtəs/, LD /ƛ́əpxts/ 'he's/she's scattering it'
TB /sčəlíqʷɫ/ 'berry', (LD, VU hadn't heard this word, used
/sʔáɫtəŋ/ 'berry')
In reviewing the field notes I notice that VU is more likely to apply
this rule when LD was not present, i.e., when he alone was responsible
for reporting the Samish form. For example, VU alone July 12, 1984
/náqʷɫ/ [nɔ́qʷɫ] 'asleep', but June 12, 1985 VU /náqʷəɫ/, LD /náqʷɫ/
'asleep'. In a few places he gave forms without the /ə/-deletion
as Saanich and forms with deletion as Samish. For example, VU Saanich
/čékʷət/, VU Samish /čékʷt/ 'wash it'. If this is indeed a difference between Saanich and Samish, then VU may have let this effect
of a Saanich accent slip into his Samish when LD was present and
giving what he said was real pure Samish.

9. no attestations

10. VU /páwiʔ ~ páwəy̓/ 'flounder (the fish)'
/páyšəč̓/ 'fir cone, pine cone'
/č̓əliʔ ~ č̓éləy̓/ 'bark of fir or balsam'

11. Historically, it is not clear whether the echo vowel was
present in Proto-Central Salish and lost in some languages or absent
in Proto-Central Salish and added in some languages (Galloway 1982:81,84,
109 proposes that both may have happened in different forms). More
examples need to be found to tell whether Samish has a synchronic rule
adding echo vowels or not.

12. see also the examples for 10, above.

13., 14., 15. no further examples to add.

16. LD /sŋəsélənəxʷ ~ sŋəsélŋəxʷ/, VU /sŋəsélŋəxʷ/ 'butter'

LD /ʔəɬtélənəxʷ/, VU /ʔəɬtélŋəxʷ/, TB /ʔeɬtélŋəxʷ ~ ʔeɬtélənəxʷ/
 'person'
LD /stélənəxʷ/, VU /stélŋəxʷ/ 'medicine'
LD /ŋə́nŋənəʔ/, VU, TB /ŋə́nəŋənəʔ/ 'sons and daughters, many offspring'

   17. /x̣əx̣áʔčeʔ/ 'small lake' vs. /x̣áčeʔ/ 'lake'
LD /stitiqiwáɬ/, VU /stitiqíwaɬ/ 'colt' (vs. VU /stiqíw/ 'horse')
/sk̉ʷək̉ʷá(ʔ)təʔ/ 'crow' vs. /sk̉ʷtáʔ/ 'raven' vs. /sk̉ʷələk̉ʷáʔtəʔ/
 'lots of crows'
/ŋə́n stəɬtáləẃ/ [ŋə́nʔ#stəlʔtáʔləwʔ] 'lots of rivers' vs.
 /ŋə́n stáʔtaləẃ/ [ŋə́nʔ#stáʔtaʔləwʔ] 'lots of creeks' vs.
 VU /s tá ləẁ/ 'river'
LD /θəq̇θəq̇əṅ/, VU /čəq̇čəq̇əṅ/ 'it's dripping lots' vs. LD /θə́q̇əṅ/,
 VU /čə́q̇əṅ/ 'it dripped'
VU /qénqəṅ/ 'thief' vs. VU /qéṅ/ 'to steal'
VU /səlséləs/ 'lots of hands' vs. VU /séləs/ 'hand'
//p[-əl-ʔ-]íʔ-pəš=pəš// /pəɬíʔpəšpəš/ 'lots of kittens' vs.
 VU /píšpiš/ [píšpɪš] or /pə́špəš/ [pɨ́špɪš] ~ LD, VU /píš ~ pə́š/
 [píš ~ pɨ́š] 'cat' (probably < Chinook Jargon). Note the use of
 probably 'characteristic' suffixed derivational reduplication =C₁əC₂,
 probably prefixed C₁íʔ- 'diminutive' plus infixed -əl- or -ə̀l-
 '(collective) plural' plus diminutive glottalization of resonant
 (if infix is -əl-) in that order.

   18. LD /ʔíθəŋ/, VU /ʔíčəŋ/ 'get dressed' vs. LD /ʔeθéṅ/, VU
 /ʔecéṅ/ 'getting dressed'
VU /ʔə́mət/ 'sit down, sit up' vs. VU /ʔám̉ət/ 'sitting down' vs.
 VU /ʔaʔám̉ət/ 'little child sitting (up or down), sitting by oneself
 lonely' (diminutive reduplication + continuative ablaut) vs.
 VU /ʔəmáttxʷ/ 'seat somebody' (metathesis +/or ablaut and stress
 shift)
VU /t̉ə́ṅət/ 'line them up, pile them up' vs. VU /stéṅəɬ/ 'all lined
 up'
VU /ləq̇ə́sət/ 'make oneself even, line oneself up (of canoe when one
 is in it for ex., race canoe, people, etc.)' vs. VU /sléq̇əɬ/ 'even'
VU /ʔə́čəqsət/ 'dodge something' (-sət 'purposive reflexive, full
 control') vs. VU /ʔəyéqt/ 'change something' (-t 'purposive full
 control transitivizer')
/kʷə́nət/ 'grab it' vs. /kʷənét/ 'taking it, holding it'
 (the last four examples show 'durative aspect')
VU /čsə́təŋsən/ 'I got hit (by something thrown)' vs. VU /čə́stəŋsən/
 'I'm getting hit'
/sx̣ə́t/ 'push it' vs. /sə́x̣t/ 'pushing it' ('continuative aspect' is
 shown in the last two [and others above] by stress shift + metathesis)

19. see examples in 2, 5, and 17 above.

20. LD /θə́əx̣tn/, VU /c̓ə́x̣tən/ 'poison [nominal]' vs. LD /θə́əx̣tənít/, VU /c̓ə́x̣tənít/ 'to poison someone'
/míłə/ 'to spirit dance' vs. VU /miłəhéw̓txʷ ~ miłəʔéw̓txʷ/, LD /miłəhéw̓xʷ/ 'spirit dance house'
/q̓ʷəyíləš/ 'to dance' vs. VU /q̓ʷəyíləšewtxʷ/, LD /q̓ʷəyíləšewxʷ/ 'dance hall' (note the strong root stress on /í/ does not change even in the presence of stress-attracting //=éw̓txʷ//)
/ƛ̓pélqə́n̓/ 'down feather' vs. /sƛ̓pélqn/ 'feather bed' vs. VU /sƛ̓íƛ̓pelqən̓/, LD /sƛ̓pélqən̓/ 'cushion' (note 'diminutive' C₁í- attracts stress away from stressed derivational suffix =élqən) (note 'diminutive' glottalization of /n̓/ in both 'down feather' and 'cushion')

3. MORPHOLOGY

3.0. Introduction

   This chapter will describe some of the morphological systems which
I have been able to discover from the data so far. Because the data
is sometimes incomplete or inconclusive I will begin with a sample of
most of the paradigms I have obtained so far. That will be followed
by a discussion of the pronominal system, verb inflections (other
than pronominal), the nominal system, the demonstrative system, the
numerals, lexical affixes, and the particle system. All forms are
given in phonemic transcription from here on, unless noted.

3.1. Some Samish Paradigms
(by Victor Underwood [VU] unless noted LD [Lena Daniels] or TB [Tommy Bob])
(lines without page numbers occur on the next field notebk. page number listed)

čə́stəŋsən	I'm getting hit
čə́stəŋ(sxʷ)	you're getting hit
čə́stəŋ	he's getting hit
čə́stəŋɫtə	we're getting hit
čə́stəŋsxʷélə	you folks are getting hit p.8
contrast:	
čsə́təŋsən	I got hit (by s-th thrown); they hit me p.8
čə́snəxʷ	hit it (accidentally, by throwing) p.16

nə tén	my mother
ʔən skʷéʔ ṅ tén	your (own) mother
skʷéʔs téns	his (own) mother
niɫ kʷə ténɫtə	(that's) our mother
niɫ kʷṅ ténhelə?	(that's) you folks' mother p.13

ʔə́w nə skʷéʔ [VU,LD]	it's my own
ʔə́wən skʷéʔ [VU,LD]	it's yours (sg.)(your own)
ʔə́w skʷéʔs kʷə? [VU,LD]	it's his p.100
skʷéʔs ʔéỉŋ [VU,LD]	it's his house
skʷéʔs sə́wniɫ [VU]	it's hers
skʷéʔs θə́wniɫ ʔéỉŋ [LD]	it's her house
skʷéʔɫ ʔéỉŋ [VU,LD]	it's our house
skʷélaʔs ʔéỉŋ [VU], skʷélaʔs ʔéỉŋ [LD]	it's their house
ʔə́wən skʷéʔən (?)éləŋ [VU], ʔə́wṅ skʷén ʔéỉəŋ [LD]	it's your own house p.102

ʔə́w-léŋnəxʷsənsə?	I'll see you (sic for him)
ʔə́w-leŋnáŋələsənsə? kʷə	we'll see you (sic for I'll see you pl.) p.16

skʷéy kʷənə sléŋnəxʷ   I can't see it
skʷéy kʷən̓ sléŋnəxʷ   you can't see it
skʷéy kʷn̓ sléŋnəxʷelə   we can't **see** it [sic for you folks can't see it]
skʷéy kʷs léŋnəxʷs   he can't see it   p.18

wét kʷə léŋnəxʷ kʷə swə́ẏqə?   who sees the man?
wét kʷə swə́ẏqə? kʷə léŋənəs   who does the man see?
wét kʷə leŋtíxʷ   who are you looking at?
ʔəw̓ nił kʷə céʔe swə́ẏəqə? (kʷə) leŋít   that's the man that sees it
  (prob. sic for 'that's the man that's watching it')
nił kʷə céʔe swə́ẏəqə? léŋnəxʷən   that's the man I saw
nił kʷə tíẏe swə́ẏəqə? leŋətín   this is the man I'm watching
nił kʷə tíẏe swə́ẏəqə? leŋətíxʷ   "   "   "   " you're   "
nił kʷə tíẏe swə́ẏəqə? leŋətís   "   "   "   " he's   "
nił kʷə tíẏe swə́ẏəqə? leŋətíłtə   "   "   "   " we're   "
nił kʷə tíẏe swə́ẏəqə? leŋətíxʷelə "   "   "   " you folks **are** watching

ʔəw̓ leŋnánəs   he sees me
ʔəw̓ léŋnəŋsxʷ   he sees you   p.20
ʔəw̓ léŋnəŋłtə   he sees us
ʔəw̓ léŋnəŋsxʷèlə   he sees you folks   p.21
láʔa kʷə léŋnəxʷəs [VU], luw kʷə léŋnəxʷs [LD]   he sees them   p.30

ʔəw leŋísəsən [VU], ʔəw̓ leŋís·n [LD]   I'm looking at you   p.102
leŋítsən [VU], ləŋítsn [LD]   I'm looking at it   p.95
...ʔəw̓ leŋítáłxʷ   (looking at us)
skʷéy kʷn̓s yásu léŋətałxʷ   you can't always look at us
kʷéʔetałxʷ   leave us alone   Text: Maiden of Deception Pass

ʔəŋáʔs   give it to me
ʔəŋáʔsəsənsə?   I'm going to give it to you
ʔəŋáʔt   to give s-th to him   p.21

təłnáŋətsxʷ   you understand it   p.20
seẏsiẏnáŋətsən   I scared myself   p.25
(cp. séẏsiẏ   I got scared   p.25)

ʔəyéqt   change s-th
ʔéčəqsət   dodge s-th   p.24
pxʷísət [VU], pxʷíst [LD]   brush oneself off
leŋəsát [VU,LD]   take care of oneself (sic? taking?)(√leŋ- 'look/see')
leŋásətsxʷ [VU], leŋástsxʷ [LD]   take care of yourself(:)
kʷənəŋítəl   they're helping each other   p.30

qʷíx̣ʷət [VU], qʷíx̣ʷt [LD]   miss it; move it
qʷíx̣ʷnəxʷ [VU, LD]   he missed it

máčt [VU, LD]   aim it
smáṁaytŋ [VU], smáṁaytŋ [LD]   it was aimed p.88 (passive)
 (vs. middle voice, homophonous):
  łx̣ásŋ   paint oneself on the face p.24

x̣élət [VU, LD]   write it
x̣éltəs [VU], x̣élts [LD]   he's writing it
kʷł sx̣éləłstəs [VU], kʷł sx̣éləłsts [LD]   he's got it written down
x̣éléls [VU,LD]   he's a writer
x̣éʔels [VU,LD]   the Transformer
x̣éléla? [LD], x̣éléla? [VU]   writing p.97

čx̣ǝt [VU,LD]   tear it
čx̣ǝtsən   I tore it
čǝx̣tsən [VU,LD] I'm tearing it, I'm splitting it (canoe with wedge for ex.)
čǝx̣náx̣ʷsən ʔəl [VU,LD]   I split it by accident, I happened to split it,
   I (finally) managed to split it p.98

ʔésə [VU], ʔés [LD]   it's me
nákʷ [VU,LD]   it's you (sg.)
níł [VU,LD]   it's him, it's her, that's it, that's the one
łníŋəł [VU,LD]   it's us
nəkʷíliye? [VU,LD]   it's you folks
nəní?łiye? [LD], nəní?łiye? [VU]   it's (lots of) them

ʔésŋ mén ~ ʔésə ʔəṅ mén [VU], ʔésəṅ mén [LD]   I'm your father

nəsx̌í?sxʷ [VU,LD]   I like you (like a friend)

ʔéwənə nə sx̣čít [VU,LD]   I don't know it/him/her
ʔéwənə ṅə sx̣əčtéŋ [VU,LD]   you don't know me
ʔéwənə ṅə sx̣əčtéŋł [VU,LD]   you don't know us
ʔéwənə ṅ x̣čít θəẇníł [VU,LD]   you don't know him p.100

kʷán·əs·xʷ [LD,VU]   you grabbed me
kʷánəsəsn [VU], kʷánəs·n [LD]   I grabbed you
kʷánətsn [LD,VU]   I grabbed him/her
kʷənésəsən(h)elə [VU], kʷánəs·ənelə [LD]   I grabbed you folks
kʷənətálxʷ [LD,VU]   you grabbed us p.102
kʷəníteŋ   she was grabbed Text: Maiden of Deception Pass

xʷc̓sást [VU], xʷə̓sást [LD]   hit s-o in the face p.102
xʷc̓sástəŋsn [VU], xʷə̓sástəŋsn [LD]   he hit me in the face (actually pass-
    ive: I was hit by s-o in the face)
c̓əl̓c̓sástŋ̓łtə [VU], ə̓əl̓ə̓sástŋ̓ł [LD]   he hit us all in the face (passive)
    p.103

kʷənŋátnəsəŋsn [LD]   he ran after me (passive)
kʷənŋátnəsnáŋəsən [LD]   I ran after you (/sn/ prob. sic for /s/)
kʷənŋátnəs [LD,VU]   he ran after him (/s/ poss. sic for /s·/)
kʷənŋátnəséŋł [LD]   he ran after us (passive: we were run after)
kʷənŋátnəsł [LD]   they ran after you folks (sic? for we ran
                                          after them) p.103

ʔíθəŋ [LD], ʔíc̓əŋ [VU]   get dressed
ʔeθéŋ́ [LD], ʔecéŋ́ [VU]   he's getting dressed p.94
ʔəθéŋəstxʷ [LD], ʔəc̓éŋəstxʷ [VU]   to dress s-o
ʔəθéŋíʔstxʷ [LD], ʔəc̓éŋíʔstxʷ [VU]   to dress him (a child)(sic? dressing)
láʔa kʷə ʔəθéŋəstəs tə ʔíŋəs [LD]   she dressed her grandson
láʔa kʷə ʔəc̓éŋəstŋ ʔə ƛ̓ méli [VU]   he was dressed by Mary
láʔa kʷə ʔəc̓éŋəstŋ ʔə ƛ̓ méli ʔə θə ʔíŋəs [VU] Mary dressed her grandson
    p.103

Miscellaneous combinations from VU text: The Maiden of Deception Pass
nə sƛ̓íʔ kʷənəs c̓táləs ʔə́ sən̓ ŋénaʔ   I want to marry your daughter
ʔn sƛ̓íʔ kʷsu ʔéłəs ʔə łníŋəł   I want that she is with us
ʔə́sə ʔənáʔsétsən ʔn̓ sʔíłənhélə   I'm the one supplying you folks' food
láʔa kʷ(?)əw̓ c̓əxʷíŋətəxʷ   you're helping them
háʔsʔəsxʷ ʔí ʔáwəs ʔáŋəs ʔə sən̓ ŋénaʔ if you don't give me your daughter
háʔsəs kʷəč̓ə́ (or háʔsəʔ skʷəč̓é) ʔáwəs ʔáŋəs ʔə sn̓ ŋénaʔ? ʔi ...
    if you don't give me your daughter then ...
(From text of speech by TB:)
háʔsənseʔ ʔə́wə syéʔ šák̓ʷŋ̓ ʔi tsássn   if I don't go bathe then I'm poor

3.2. Pronouns

There appear to be seven sets of pronouns in Samish, falling into four
categories: pronominal verbs, possessive pronouns, subject pronouns, and
object pronouns. Each has two subtypes, except for pronominal verbs.

3.2.1. Pronominal verbs (called predicative pronominals in Montler 1984).

These independent words can be used as independent subject or object
pronouns (for emphasis) or as verbs (and can be inflected like verbs to
a limited degree). As verbs they have an emphatic sense too, 'it is I
(that does X)', etc.; the semantic force is probably one of focus.
To express 'he, him' and 'she, her' demonstrative pronouns are used

in much the same way; they are discussed under demonstratives. It seems
likely that the 3rd person plural form listed below for VU and LD
has a demonstrative root as well.

	singular	plural
1st person	TB ʔése,VU ʔə́sə, LD ʔə́s	ɬníŋəɬ
2nd person	nə́kʷ	nəkʷíl̓iye̓ʔ
3rd person	níɬ	VU nəní̓ʔɬiye̓ʔ, LD nəníʔɬiye̓ʔ,
		TB hé·ɬtən, VU héʔeɬtən

  Besides the example given in 3.1 above, there are in texts:
TB nə šxʷ(č)əlé tíye, ʔése. 'This is where I belong, me.'
VU ʔə́sə ʔəŋáʔséʔt–sən ʔn̓ s=ʔíɬən–hélə. 'I am the one supplying
  you folks' food.' (note double stresses for emphasis as well)
VU ʔn̓ šx̣íʔ kʷsu ʔéɬes ʔə ɬníŋəɬ. 'I want her here with us.'
VU níɬ–su yéʔ–s ʔáx̣ʷ ʔə tə s=ʔəl–ʔéləxʷ–s. 'So he went to go to
  her parents.'
TB ʔi čəčétəs hé·ɬtn tíye x̣péy̓ snə́xʷəɬ. nəxʷsčéy hé·ɬtn.
  'They fixed this cedar canoe. They were canoe builders. (talking
  about many people, tribes, especially the Samish)

3.2.2. Possessive pronouns.

  These suffixes and preposed particles (or prefixes) are added
adjacent to nominals to show personal possession. When a verb
phrase is subordinated it can be nominalized and then possessed
to show its subject by this set of pronouns. When the 3rd person
form is attatched to a nominal and another nominal phrase follows,
the second nominal can semantically possess the first (as in English
"the web of the spider" = "the spider's web"). Those in the set
shown with a hyphen following are prefixes if no pause is heard
before the nominal following or preposed particles if a pause is
heard; they phonetically often are heard suffixed to the word
immediately preceding their nominal (often a demonstrative article).

	singular	plural
1st person	nə–	–ɬtə
2nd person	(ʔə)n̓–	(ʔə)n̓– ...–helə?
3rd person	–s	–s

  Examples are plentiful above. Note the 2nd person plural circumfix
as in VU níɬ kʷn̓ ténhelə? '(that's) you folks' mother'. Also note
how this possessive is often applied to nominal phrases as in
VU s–k̓ʷéy kʷ–n̓ s–léŋ–nəxʷ–(h)elə 'you folks can't see it'
(it's–impossible the–your nominalizer–see–(manage to/partial control

transitivizer)-(2nd person plural), lit. "you folks' managing to see it is impossible"). Notice also that -s can be translated 'his, her, its, their'. In the 2nd person pluralizer the /h/ can be optionally dropped following a consonant. Also, when the 2nd person preposed pronoun form is suffixed to a word the /ʔə/ is normally dropped (except in extra careful speech).

3.2.3. Emphatic possessive pronouns.

This set is composed of a nominalized root, skʷéʔ 'own', affixed with the possessive pronouns from the last set. These forms then are preposed to the nominal possessed or stand independently. Thus:

	singular	plural
1st person	nə skʷéʔ	skʷéɬ
2nd person	(ʔə)ń skʷéʔ	((ʔə)ń skʷéʔ ...-(h)elə probably)
3rd person	skʷéʔs	VU skʷéɫaʔs, LD skʷélaʔs

Examples above, like VU skʷéʔs səẃniɫ 'it's hers', show that the masculine or feminine demonstrative pronoun can be added; examples like LD skʷéʔs θəẃniɫ ʔéłŋ 'it's her house' show that these can even precede and modify nominals. They are also often preceded by the particle /ʔəẃ/ which emphasizes contrast with preceding information (see examples in 3.1), and they can be used with normal possessives for even more emphasis, as in VU ʔəẃəń skʷéʔəń (ʔ)éłəŋ, LD ʔəẃəń skʷéń ʔéłəŋ 'it's your own house'.

3.2.4. Object pronouns with purposeful control transitivizer, //-(ə)t//.

This set is suffixed following the transitivizer. Before the 1st person sg. and the 2nd person (sg. and pl.) and the reflexive the /t/ is lost. This is a consequence of an old merger in Proto-Central Salish and consequent phonological changes. There the transitivizer's *t plus the initial *s in these suffixes became *c (a portmanteau containing parts of two morphemes). Historical sound changes occurred so that *c remains in most Central Salish languages (including Clallam), becomes /θ/ in Halkomelem, Mainland Comox, probably in Pentlatch, and in many words in Saanich, and becomes /s/ in the rest of Northern Straits and in some words in Saanich (Thompson, Thompson and Efrat 1974 and Galloway 1982). Thus the morphophonemic rule that the /t/ of this transitivizer is lost before the Samish object pronouns /-s/ and /-sə/ and the reflexive.

	singular	plural		
1st person	-s	-áłxʷ	reflexive:	-sət
			reciprocal:	- əł

```
2nd person   -sə          -sə(-subj.)-(h)elə
3rd person   zero         zero
```

Notice the separate 2nd person plural form. It is a circumfix in
the sense that it surrounds the subject affix ending. Actually
-(h)elə on the end is a pluralizer also used with the 2nd pl. subject
pronouns and possessive pronouns in Samish. It is reported for Saanich
also (Montler 1984:218-9) but there as a postposed particle rather
than a suffix. In the Samish example, VU /kʷənésəsən(h)elə/,
LD /kʷénəs·ənelə/ 'I grabbed you folks', notice that when LD drops
the /ə/ in -sə (which VU keeps), morphophonemic rule 1 applies to
convert the second /s/ to length. Thus it seems that -sən '1st
person sg. independent subject pronoun' here is a suffix rather
than a particle as in Saanich. Similarly, LD's /elə/ is also a
suffix here because no vowel initial words are attested in Samish.
It may be that VU uses -(h)elə as a particle when he pronounces it
with the /h/ (/h/ inserted epenthetically to prevent an initial
vowel) and uses it as a suffix when he omits the /h/. Montler's
citations of the morpheme in Saanich always show it beginning with
/h/.

-təİ has an allomorph -átəl which occurs in forms like lənátəl
'looking after one another' (continuative aspect).

Some syntactic notes here. When a transitive verb is inflected for
both 3rd person object and 3rd person subject and only one nominal
phrase follows, that NP is the object, never the subject. When two NP's
follow such a verb, the order is V S O. When one NP follows a transitive
verb with non-3rd person object, that NP is the subject. When one NP
follows an intransitive verb that NP is subject unless preceded by ʔə
'oblique case'. For examples see the text in 5.3 below.

3.2.5. Object pronouns with other transitivizers.

	singular	plural	reflexive with -nəxʷ: -áŋət
1st person	-áŋəs	-áɫxʷ	(perhaps reciprocal with -nəxʷ: -əwəl)
2nd person	-áŋə	-áŋələ ?	
3rd person	zero	zero	

In the few examples I have these suffixes retain stress when the root
and its other affixes have a weak or neutral (variable) stress valence
(√leŋ 'see'), and lose it when the root or other affixes have a strong
stress valence (√kʷén 'grab, hold, take'). This set of suffixes is
attested with the following Samish transitivizers, -nəxʷ 'non-control
transitive (happen to, manage to, accidentally do something to someone)'
-stəxʷ 'causative', -nəs '(purposive control) transitive', and -əs
'(effort) transitive'. These transitivizers will be discussed in 3.3
below. Two of them, -nəxʷ and -stəxʷ, lose /əxʷ/ in certain morphological environments:

  -nəxʷ -› -n before 'reflexive' -áŋət (and probably before
     -əwəl ~ -əkʷəl 'reciprocal')
  -stəxʷ -› -st before '3rd person subject' -əs or '3rd person sub-
     ordinate subject' -s.

Notice that, unlike in Saanich, -nəxʷ is attested in examples before
3rd person subject suffixes. For example, in VU's text, the Maiden of
Deception Pass:

kʷén·əxʷəs tə sčé·nəxʷ ʔəẃ stéŋ ʔəl̓, cəẃ mák̓ʷ stéŋ ƛ̓iƛ̓əč ʔéɫe,
 kʷsə ƛ̓iƛ̓əč sʔiɫən. 'They get the fish, anything/whatever, everything at the [sea] bottom right here, the sea-bottom food.' (see
 text for word-by-word translation, in section 5), and
niɫsuʔ léŋnəxʷs kʷsə sƛ̓éləqəm ʔéɫe kʷs ʔiʔəƛ̓iƛ̓əč. 'So then
 she sees/saw a powerful monster right here on the sea bottom.', and
liɫəq ʔəl̓ kʷs kʷén·əxʷs tə sʔiɫən čsəléʔe kʷs ʔiʔəƛ̓iƛ̓əč. 'It
 was just easy for them to get the food from down there at the bottom.'
 (the subordinate clauses begin with kʷs here).

The other transitivizers have not yet been found with a reflexive,
but the loss of /əxʷ/ from the 'causative' is attested in examples like:

LD láʔa kʷə ʔəθéŋəstəs tə ʔiŋəs. 'She dressed her grandson.'
VU kʷɫ sx̣éləɫstəs, LD kʷɫ sx̣éləɫsts 'he's got it written down'
VU x̣əɫáʔasts ʔə cə ʔəẃ mák̓ʷ stéŋ sʔiɫən. 'He's feeding them
 every kind of food.'

The '2nd person plural object' form is only attested once so far,
but appears to have an unstressed allomorph, -ələ, of the normal 2nd

person pluralizer, -élə. Thus,

VU ʔəẃ leŋnáŋələsənsəʔ kʷə 'I'll see you folks'

This form was glossed in my notes as 'we'll see you', but an examination
of the tape showed that "we'll" was misheard for "I'll" and 'you (pl.)'
was intended; I was asking for one way to say goodbye to VU and his wife
and had already asked for and gotten 'I'll see you (sg.)'.

3.2.6. Non-subordinate subject pronouns.

These are used for the main verb in a sentence (usually the first
word). The main verb precedes any subordinate clauses. Evidence has
been given above that these pronouns are often suffixes. They are
also attested phonologically postposed to the verb (for example, after
(-)səʔ 'future tense'). Thus I have shown them with a parenthesized
affix marker, (-). The 3rd person form is only suffixed, - ∅ with intransitives.

	singular	plural
1st person	(-)s-ən	VU (-)ɬtə, LD (-)ɬ
2nd person	(-)s-xʷ	(-)s-xʷ-elə
3rd person	-əs, -∅	-əs, -∅

The segmented (-)s- indicates 'non-subordinate subject/main verb subject'.
It is cognate with -č in most other Central Salish languages (-c in Halkomelem), serving the same function. Notice LD's normally reduced form of
the 1st person plural form. It is attested in a number of examples, like:

LD kʷənŋátnəsəŋɬ 'he ran after us' (lit. passive: 'we were run after')
LD léwəɬ kʷə tíqʷənəxʷ, VU láʔaɬtə kʷə tíqʷənəxʷ 'we hit it' (the
  first word is a past tense auxiliary which takes the main verb subject
  inflection)
LD ėəlėsástŋ̇ɬ, VU ėəlėsástŋ̇ɬtə 'he hit us all in the face' (passive
  again)(rare attestation of VU /ė/)

3.2.7. Subordinate subject pronouns.

These are much like the last set but without the (-)s- marker. They
all appear to be true suffixes phonologically (note the lack of initial
consonant in most of them). When preceded by a stressed vowel the
initial schwas drop.

	singular	plural
1st person	-ən	VU -ɬtə, LD -ɬ
2nd person	-əxʷ	-əxʷelə

3rd person   -əs   -əs

   This set is mainly (if not exclusively) attested in the data as subjects of subordinate relative clauses modifying a preceding nominal phrase. For example,

VU níɫ kʷə tíye swə́ẏəqə? leŋətín. 'This is the man I'm watching.'
 (a complete paradigm with this sentence appears above in 3.1)
VU níɫ kʷə cé?e swə́ẏəqə? léŋnəxʷən. 'That's the man I saw.'
VU wa?áčə (?)əẇ kʷəns txʷənétəṅ kʷṅs yi?áx̣ʷ ?ə kʷ sé?enəṅ
 sən sčélə(?)če? lá?a kʷəẇ čəxʷíŋətəxʷ. 'I guess that's the way
 you're being taken, going toward where your (female) relatives are
 at whom you were helping.' (see word-for-word translation in text
 of the Maiden of Deception Pass)
VU wét kʷə leŋtíxʷ. 'Who are you looking at?'

3.3. Verb inflections.

   Besides the subject and object pronoun inflections above, verbs in Samish are attested so far inflected for the following:

3.3.1. Transitive.
 -ət 'purposeful control transitive',
 -nəxʷ 'non-control transitive',
 -stəxʷ 'causative control transitive',
 -nəs '(purposive control) transitive', and
 -əs '(effort) transitive'
 (these are also called control suffixes because they express the degree
 of control the subject has over the action; -nəxʷ and -stəxʷ have allomorphs -náx̣ʷ and -stáx̣ʷ respectively for weak-stress valenced roots
 without underlying vowels as Montler points out for Saanich)

3.3.2. Intransitive.
 -əlá? 'structured activity (non-continuative/non-actual aspect)',
 -éls 'structured activity (continuative/actual aspect)'
 (these are allomorphs of a single suffix which could almost be analyzed as
 being inflected itself for aspect in the same way most verbs are, by
 stress shift and metathesis!),
 -sət 'reflexive' could be included here because when not preceded by
 control transitivizer -ət it produces semantic intransitives (has
 allomorphs -sát and -ésət after different roots which are weak-stress
 valenced and lacking underlying vowels, as Montler points out for Saanich)
 -əŋ 'intransitive' (compare q̓ʷél 'get ripe, cooked', q̓ʷél-ət 'cook (barbe-
 cue/roast) it' with q̓ʷéləṅ 'he's barbecuing')

3.3.3. Beneficiary (= Montler's "factives").

-si 'benefactive/malefactive',

-ŋi ~ -ŋə 'indirectly affected object'

(these affixes are cognate with affixes with the same function in other
Salish languages, including Halkomelem [Galloway 1977:250-260], and
Thompson [Thompson and Thompson forthcoming]; Montler 1984, follows
Thompson and Thompson in using the terms 'indirective' and 'relational'
for the Saanich cognates). Both these suffixes precede transitivizers.

3.3.4. Aspect.

'continuative' aspect is expressed by what Montler calls radical
morphological processes in Saanich; in Samish the following processes
are attested so far: reduplication (both prefixed and infixed),
infixing (both of reduplication and of /ʔ/), ablaut (several kinds),
metathesis (several kinds), stress shift, consonant shifting, and
vowel deletion; words in 'non-continuative' aspect are generally
the base forms on which the 'continuative' and other radical inflectional processes operate; thus the following processes can express
'continuative' aspect in Samish:

C_1ə- prefixed reduplication (C_1 = the first root consonant)

-C_1ə- reduplication infixed after V_1 (the first root vowel)

k^w,č -> w,y respectively in affixed continuative reduplication (this
   rule precedes ʔ-infixing)

é -> á (-Aá- /é_ or á-ablaut)

ə́ -> é (-Aé- /ə́_ or é-ablaut)

íCə, áCə -> əCé (-Aé- /(í,á)Cə_ or é-ablaut)(few exx.)

-ʔ- infixed after a stressed root vowel (/V̆V́_)
   additional infixing can occur after this rule, i.e.,
   V́$_1$-ʔ-C$_2$ -> V́$_1$ʔV$_1$C$_2$ (an echo vowel)
   V́$_1$-ʔ-C$_2$ -> əʔV́$_1$C$_2$ (əʔ inserted before V́ instead of ʔ after)
   V́$_1$-ʔ-# -> V́$_1$ʔə# (ə is added when the stressed vowel is root-final)
     (in these three statements the V and C can be later in the root than
     the first vowel and second consonant)

-ʔ- infixed after non-initial resonants (/(C,V)R_)(infixation after
   more than one resonant in a stem is optional; speakers can even differ
   as to which resonant is chosen)

√C$_1$C$_2$ə́ -> C$_1$ə́C$_2$ (prefixes can precede such metathesis, for ex. x^w-)

√V̆V́$_1$C$_2$V$_2$ -> V$_1$C$_2$V́$_2$ (stress shift in the opposite direction from the
   metathesis just above)

C$_1$ə́C$_2$-əlaʔ -> C$_1$(ə)C$_2$-éls (this may just be the working of stress
   valence rules with a strong-valenced suffix, but if not, it may
   be a pattern separate from the aspect-marked suffixes here)

ə -> zero (is dropped) /C$_2$-ʔ-_C$_3$ (attested in one example, ɬə́mx^w
   'raining' vs. ɬə́məx^w 'rain (non-continuative)')

some of these co-occur with each other with particular roots, but this
   does not intensify the continuative meaning;

zero   there are a few roots (such as yéʔ 'go, go to') which can be
  translated either continuative or non-continuative without any
  inflectional difference
the distribution of these inflections can be predicted partly
  on the basis of phonological environments and partly on morphemic
  classes as in Saanich (Montler 1984:112-130). There are some
  differences in morphemes, environments, continuative allomorphs,
  and analysis between Saanich and Samish dialects. In both however,
  'continuative' aspect expresses an on-going action continuing at
  a past, present or future time specified by the context. Before giving
  the inflections for the other Samish aspects here are some examples
  of non-continuative/continuative contrasts.

non-continuative--continuative examples:
ʔíɫən--ʔíʔɫəṅ, ʔámət--ʔámət (dim. + cont. ʔaʔámət p.5 field notes),
qʷél--qʷáqʷəl, pék̇ʷŋ--pəpék̇ʷŋ̇, csátən--cə́stəṅ, ɫáməxʷ--ɫə́mxʷ,
štéṅ--sə́təṅ (šəštəṅásəṅ 'he's walking around'), (spxʷə́laʔ)--
pəxʷéls, q̇ʷələŋ--q̇ʷələṅ, kʷéčŋ--kʷəkʷéčŋ, téẏəsət--téẏtəsət (ʔ),
čáq̇ʷŋ--čáʔq̇ʷŋ̇, yéʔ--yéʔ, stéṅ--stéṅ (p.20--p.30), mílačəsən--
ʔesmíʔiləčəs, c̣q̇əṅ--c̣ə́q̇əṅ, ʔ--héɫxəẇe (h ~ ʔ), ɫtáxtŋ--ɫə́txtŋ,
q̇ʷəyíləš--q̇ʷəyíləš ~ q̇ʷəyíləš, ʔ--xʷəxʷə́ẏim (i or ə),
ləhél--ləhéʔel̇, ʔ--tétəẏ, (s-x̣tə́k̇ʷŋ)--x̣ə́tk̇ʷŋ, q̇áwət--q̇awétṅ
(cont. + result.ʔ), (sə́ɫq̇ʷ)--sɫə́q̇ʷt, ʔ--təq̇áʔst, psə́q̇ʷt--pə́sq̇ʷt
(LD reverses glosses), číq--čéẏəq (ʔ), kʷíntəl--kʷíẇəntəl,
náčən--nənə́yəṅ, xʷčə́t--xʷə́ẏt, čák̇ʷəsət--čáẇst, ʔəné--ʔiʔəné́ʔə,
x̣ʷáŋ--x̣ʷəʔáṅ, ʔíθəŋ--ʔeθéṅ, tíq̇ʷənəxʷ--tíʔq̇ʷət, ɫəltást--ɫəltást,
čx̣ʷáɫs--čx̣ʷáʔɫs, ɫátəm (mʔ)--ɫéʔtəm, qén--qéqəṅ, qʷél--qʷáqʷəl
(cont. + result. qʷəqʷél p.95)--qʷə́lqʷəl (char.)--qʷə́lqʷəl,
qék̇ʷəŋ--(sqíʔqəẇ), ɫáp--VU ɫáɫəṗ ~ LD ɫáɫṗ, šák̇ʷŋ (šišk̇ʷám dim.
--šiləšk̇ʷám dim. + pl.)--šišk̇ʷáʔam, VU,TB tíləm--LD tíləm ~ VU tətíləm,
kʷsátəs--kʷə́st[əs], kʷsén--kʷə́sṅ, čtéŋ--čə́tŋ, ɫə́k̇ʷələʔ--ɫ̇kʷéls,
ɫpə́xt--ɫə́pxtəs, x̣ə́ləlaʔ--x̣əlél̇s, x̣čə́t--x̣ə́čt, čx̣ét (čəx̣náxʷ p.98)
--čə́x̣t, sx̣ə́t--sə́x̣t, xʷq̇ṗə́t--xʷq̇ə́ṗt, (təkʷnáxʷ p.98) tkʷə́t--ʔ,
háq̇ʷnəxʷ--háʔq̇ʷnəxʷ, kʷə́nət--kʷə́nét (cont. + persis.)--kʷə́nésəṅ
(non-cont. + effort trans. + persis.ʔ)--kʷə́nésəṅ (cont. + effort +
persis.ʔ), čák̇ʷs--čaʔáẇəs (+ effort trans.), sékʷəs (LD sékʷs)--
seʔéẇəs, ʔá·ɫ--VU ʔáʔaləɫ ~ LD ʔáʔaɫɫ (pl.), LD ʔítt--LD ʔíʔtt,
síɫəŋ--səsíɫəṅ, ʔ--səséẇt, téẏəq (təléẏəq pl.)--tətéẏəq.
(Forms in parentheses have additional inflections; glosses see 4.1 Verbs.)

other aspect inflections:
-Aí- /-...ə_ 'persistent' aspect (as Montler 1984:54-56 notes for Saanich,
  this affix replaces /ə/ with /í/ in the rightmost suffix not preceded
  by a suffix with a non-schwa vowel; the meaning expressed is one of
  an action continued past inception to a state (examples above + below);

the 'durative' aspect in the Musqueam dialect of Downriver Halkomelem
(Suttles 1980) appears cognate in form and function but appears to
travel rightward only to the end of the stem, not rightward even into
inflectional endings as in Saanich and Samish.

-Aá- ~ -Aé- /V...ə_ 'resultive' aspect (examples above + below),
emphasizes the result of a verbal action, apparently occurs also
(as an infix) in roots which lack a vowel elsewhere

ʔəs- ~ s- 'stative' aspect (examples below), ʔəs- has a wider distribution than in Saanich

-əł 'durative' aspect (examples below), may rather be an allomorph of
'stative' aspect, seldom if ever attested without a stative meaning
even when not co-occuring with the 'stative' prefix

examples:

ʔíθəŋ 'get dressed', ʔeθéŋ 'getting dressed', ʔəθénəstəs 'she dressed
someone' ('causative' + 'resultive'), ʔəθeŋíʔstxʷ 'to dress him (a
child)' ('persistent' + 'resultive' + 'continuative'? + 'causative'),
(these forms from LD; VU replaces θ with c throughout), VU ʔəćénəstŋ
kʷəʔ '(t)he(y) dressed him up' ('resultive' + 'causative' + 'passive')

LD x̌čétsxʷ 'you figure it out', VU ʔəw̓ x̌čítsxʷ kʷəʔ kʷə sɬéniʔ
'you know the woman' (kʷəʔ roughly 'anyway')(//x̌č-ə[-Aí-]t-sxʷ// with
'persistent' ablaut on the 'purposive control transitive' suffix, -ət,
VU láʔa kʷ ʔəw̓ x̌əčsís 'he knows me' (//√x̌əč-s-ə[-Aí-]s// with
'persistent' ablaut on the '3rd person subject' suffix)

VU léŋnəxʷ 'see someone' (with 'non-control transitive'), VU léŋətaɬxʷ
'look at us' (with 'purposive control transitive'), VU niɬ kʷə tíye
swéy̓əqəʔ leŋətíxʷelə 'this is the man you folks are watching'
('persistent' ablaut on the '2nd person pl. subordinate subject' suffix)

VU,LD sqílŋ (√səq=íl-əŋ) 'go outside' (-íl 'inceptive, go, come, get';
-əŋ 'middle voice'), VU,LD ʔəséqɬ 'be outside' ('stative' + 'resultive'
+ 'durative')

VU,LD k̓ʷséŋ 'to count', VU,LD kʷɬəw̓ ʔəsk̓ʷásɬ 'it's already counted'

LD ʔítt 'to sleep', VU,LD ʔətátŋ̓ 'sleepy'

VU tés 'to approach, get near', VU stésəɬ (LD stésɬ) 'be near'

LD sk̓ʷəɬk̓ʷéθ̓ (VU sk̓ʷəɬk̓ʷéc̓) 'real crooked' (s- 'stative' + Cıə- prob.
'durative' + 'pl.' infix -əɬ-), LD sk̓ʷáθ̓ɬ (VU sk̓ʷác̓ɬ) 'crooked
(of tree, road, canoe, person, etc.)', VU yéʔ k̓ʷəc̓əsət 'it's going
crooked'

VU ləc̓ét 'fill it', VU sléc̓əɬ (LD sléθ̓ɬ) 'it is full'

VU,LD p̓éɬ 'get sober, come to one's senses; hatch', LD sṕáɬ·
'be sober' ('stative' + 'resultive' + 'durative')

VU,LD ʔəsʔáy̓q 'it's wrong', LD sθ̓əθ̓əwéč (VU sc̓əc̓əwéč) 'be sitting',
LD sčəwét 'be smart, know how to', LD sxʷəxʷík̓ʷtŋ 'be drunk'
(all 'stative' aspect)

VU síʔsəɬ (LD síʔsɬ) 'high', VU,LD ƛ̓éčɬ 'low' (cp. ƛ̓əč 'deep

(of water, spear in animal, etc.)'), VU náqʷəɬ (LD náqʷɬ)
'(be) asleep', LD,VU sxʷáy̓əɬ 'awake' (cp. LD,VU xʷčə́t 'wake
him up')

3.3.5. Voice.

-əŋ 'middle voice'; a verb in the middle voice by classical definition
  is one with its subject pronoun acting on or for itself without an
  object pronoun; in Samish, as in most other Salishan languages, the
  middle voice fits this definition but adds some additional variants
  (allosemes): in the semantic environment of body-part suffixes
  'middle voice' refers to the subject doing an action to or on that
  part of his own body; in the semantic environment of an inanimate
  subject (and sometimes even an animate subject) 'middle voice' can
  mean an action by the subject upon itself or as a state of being
  (adjectival, participial) developed by and upon the subject itself
  with no perceived outside agent; in some cases only an intransitiv-
  izing meaning remains; in some cases the 'middle' is crystallized
  or petrified (for example on an otherwise unattested root) and its
  original semantic contribution to the present gloss is only suspected.
-əŋ 'passive voice'; in the Samish passive the patient is acted upon
  by an unspecified agent ('he was hit'), or by a 3rd person indefinite
  subject ('they hit him','he was hit by someone', 'someone hit him'), or
  by a nominal phrase preceded by the preposition (ʔə) (called the 'oblique
  case marker' in Montler 1984 and elsewhere) ('he was hit by Mary',
  'he was hit by his son', etc.); the passive suffix must be preceded
  by a transitivizer; it may be followed by a subject pronoun to
  express the semantic patient ('I was hit'); no object pronoun affixes
  can be used, and there is no separate passive paradigm as there is in
  Halkomelem; where the agent of a subordinate passive verb must be indica-
  ted 3rd person subordinate or possessive pronouns are used.
'active voice' is unmarked.

3.3.6. Mood.

'declarative' mood is unmarked.
'imperative' is seldom attested so far (7 examples), all examples but
  one show the simple use of -s-xʷ '2nd person sg. independent subject'
  (thus xʷə́ŋsxʷ 'Hurry up!', ʔə́mətsxʷ ʔaɫ 'Seat yourself.', but
  in the text by VU: kʷéʔetaɫxʷ skʷəče '(You can) leave us alone.'
  where there is no subject affix); more examples are needed to tell
  if a Samish command form exists like the Saanich post particle {čə}.
-ə 'interrogative (yes/no question)', suffixed to the first verb
  in the sentence (whether auxiliary or main verb)(thus:
  níɫ-ə céʔe sɫéni? 'Is that the woman?', ʔə̀w níɫ-ə kʷə čéʔsə?
  'Is that those two people?'), less often appears as a particle /ʔə/
  following the first verb in the sentence (thus xʷésŋ ʔə 'Is it
  soapberries?' [following the syntactic rule that sentence-initial words
  except particles become verbs, nominal xʷésŋ 'soapberry' here
  becomes an existential verb 'is a soapberry, is soapberries (generic)';
  in such a position even nominals can be inflected with subject pronouns,

possessive pronouns, and even tense, though little else inflectional],
sx̌ʷénen ʔə́ cə sémə̌ssəʔ kʷə swíltn-ə̀w̓ łqənéʔtən
'Will the Samish be the same as swíltnə̀w̓ łqənéʔtən (anchored net)?');
other interrogatives than yes/no questions (wh-questions, etc.) are formed
by special interrogative verbs including: wét 'who is it?, who is?',
stén̓ 'what is it?, what is?', k̓ʷín 'how many is it?, how many are?'
(these roots can be inflected with lexical suffixes, thus k̓ʷənéla
'how many persons are there?, how many people are?', steñáləs 'what
color is it?', etc.), ʔín̓ət 'what did someone say?', ʔəx̌én̓ kʷčsəléʔes
'where is he from?', səns 'where is it?'; as verbs this set can also be
inflected by subject pronouns, future tense, and perhaps other inflections
(for example, VU stáṅət 'do what?' seems to have ablaut + -ət transitivizer)
(Montler 1984 analyzes the Saanich cognate of this -ət as a rare 'stative')
no 'subjunctive' with negative, conditional, and contrary-to-fact verb
    phrases (unlike Halkomelem); instead there are negative verbs such as
    ʔə́wə ~ ʔáwə 'no; not be, be not', ʔə́wənə 'it is none, don't have any',
    sk̓ʷéy 'it's impossible, can't', etc. and conditional verb há?
    'if, when'; these are inflected with subject pronouns like any
    other verbs and can be followed by tense and by subordinate clauses
    (kʷə + possessive pronoun + main verb).

3.3.7. Tense.
-səʔ ~ -saʔ ~ postposed səʔ ~ saʔ 'future tense' (see examples above)
VU -ələ?, TB -ələ 'past tense' (suffixed after subject pronoun suffixes),
    found in texts only so far, for ex. VU niłsu léʔe-s-ələʔ čéʔeys
    'So that's where they were working.', TB kʷsu siyém-ələ nə
    sʔəléləxʷ, ʔi kʷəntís-ələ tiye heyí x̌čen̓ín 'So my dear deceased
    elders (or ancestors/parents), he had these big spoken thoughts/
    spoken feelings.' (note use of this past tense with the adjective
    siyém 'dear' to apply to a nominal sʔəléləxʷ 'elders' meaning
    'deceased/in the past'; this is common in other dialects too as
    in Saanich and in related languages like Halkomelem; phonologically
    -ələ? is so far attested only as a suffix not as a particle in Samish
VU láʔa, LD lə́w ~ lə̀w̓ ~ lúw̓ 'ambiguous past tense' (a sentence-initial
    auxiliary verb to which independent subject pronouns are suffixed,
    this can be followed by subordinate clauses, i.e. kʷə + main verb);
    for example: VU láʔałtə kʷə tíqʷənəxʷ, LD lə́wəłt kʷə tíqʷənəxʷ
    'We hit it (past tense).', LD,VU lə̀w̓ tə kʷł łək̓ʷǎn̓ətən 'They
    tripped him (lit. he was tripped).' (the demonstrative /tə/ is
    used here unexplainably instead of the normal /kʷə/; also VU follows
    LD in using /lə̀w̓/ here instead of his usual /láʔa/; the form LD uses
    may have the particle (ʔ)ə̀w̓ attached in these examples and may really
    have the form lə instead of ləw, lə̀w̓, etc.; note the different
    form and position of these verbs from the Saanich postposed particle
    //ləʔ// 'past' (Montler 1984:210-211). Notice that the Samish

láʔa ~ lə 'ambiguous past' is cognate in form and function with
Upriver Halkomelem /lə/ (Galloway 1977:141-142, 299-300) and like
it is occasionally also translated by the present tense (see examples
under 14 in section 3.5 below).
'present tense' is unmarked but so often is past tense since tense
  marking is optional.

3.3.8. Plural.

-C₁í-: sq̇éməɬ--sq̇əq̇íməɬ 'lots of canoe paddles (not just 3)'
        čénəs--čəčínəs 'all one's teeth' (vs. ŋə́n čénəs 'a lot of teeth')
        snéxʷəɬ--snəníxʷəɬ (LD snəníxʷɬ), ŋə́n snéxʷəɬ 'lots of canoes'
C₁əC₂-: nə́qən--nəqnə́qən 'keeps diving repeatedly'
        LD θ̇q̇éŋ (VU c̣q̇éŋ)--LD θ̇əq̇θ̇əq̇əŋ (VU c̣əq̇c̣əq̇əŋ) 'it's dripping lots'
        sɬéniʔ--sɬənɬéniʔ 'lots of women (a dozen or more)'
        ŋénəʔ--ŋənŋénəʔ 'sons and daughters'
        ṫéləẇ--ṫəlṫéləẇ 'arms'
        sṫélŋəxʷ (LD sṫéləŋəxʷ)--sṫəlṫélŋəxʷ (LD sṫəlṫéləŋəxʷ) 'lots
          of medicine'
        stáɬəẇ--stəɬtáɬəẇ 'lots of rivers'
        sčé·nəxʷ--LD sčənčé·nəxʷ (VU čénenxʷ < Saanich) 'lots of fish'
-C₁əC₂-: nə́č sṫélŋəxʷ--nə́čnəč sṫélŋəxʷ (LD sṫéləŋəxʷ) 'different medicines'
C₁ə-: méʔkʷɬ (VU méʔkʷəɬ)--LD,VU məméʔkʷɬ 'lots of people got hurt'
        šéyəɬ--šəšéyəɬ 'older siblings'
-ìə- ~ -lə- ~ -əl-: (these allomorphs are distributed as follows in Saanich:
  -ìə- /(C)Ci_C (here i -> e also)
  -lə- /(C)CV_ʔC
  -əl- /elsewhere
  In Samish there are some differences; examples follow (sg.--pl.):
  -ìə-: sáɬ--sáìəɬ 'lots of doorways/doors/roads'
        ʔéləŋ--ʔéìələŋ 'lots of houses'
        ʔá·ɬ--ʔáʔaìəɬ (LD ʔáʔaìɬ) '(lots) getting aboard (car, canoe, etc.)'
          (this also features 'continuative' infixing -ʔ-V₁-)
  -lə-: LD méʔkʷɬ (VU méʔkʷəɬ)--LD méləkʷɬ 'get hurt over and over'
          (contrast LD,VU məméʔkʷɬ 'lots of people got hurt')
        ʔ--LD séləʔst ~ səléʔsət (VU səléʔsət) 'lots of parents'
  -əl-: (ṫíləm 'sing') LD ṫíləṁ (VU ṫəṫíləṁ) 'singing'--LD,VU ṫəlíləm
          'lots singing'
        ṫéẏəq̇--ṫəléẏəq̇ 'they're all angry/mad'
        méqʷ 'thick (in girth)'--məlméqʷsət (LD məlméqʷst) tə ʔesítŋ
          'a lot of puffy clouds' (lit. 'many are getting thick + the + cloud')
          ('continuative' C₁ə- reduplication featured here too)
        séčs ('parent's sibling')--səléčs 'aunts and uncles'
        LD səẏéčn̓--səléẏčn 'younger siblings' (metathesis also?)
        šxʷáq̇ʷaʔ--šxʷəláq̇ʷaʔ 'relatives'
  -əɬ-: VU,LD sléʔɬ ~ slé·ɬ--VU,LD sléləɬ ~ VU sləléʔeɬ ~ LD səlsəléʔeɬ

'all one's in-laws'

other examples co-occur with reduplications (see 3.3.10)

(-)əC₁-: swéýqə?--VU səw·éýqə? (LD səwéýqə?) 'lots of men' (only ex.
       of an irregular type)

other irregular types co-occur with other reduplications (see below)

From the examples above it can be seen that the Samish 'plural' is only
marked when a large number or a collective group is intended; singular,
dual, and small numbers are unmarked or counted with numerals; as noted
for Halkomelem (Galloway 1977), Saanich (Montler 1984) and elsewhere
what is pluralized semantically in verbs is either the action doné or
the subject (for intransitives) or the object (for transitives); note
that nominals are inflected with the same affixes and meanings too.

3.3.9. Diminutive.

C₁ə-...-?-: x̣áče? 'lake'--x̣əx̣á?če? 'small lake'

         k̓ʷənélə 'how many persons'--k̓ʷək̓ʷənélə? 'just a few people
         (three or so)'

         ?ámət 'sitting'--?a?ámət 'little child sitting (up or
         down), sitting by oneself lonely'

         šétəŋ 'walking'--?əw̓ šəšétəŋ 'taking a little walk'

         ƛúƛa? ~ ƛəẃƛa? 'small'--ƛəƛəẃƛa? 'a few small ones'
         (could be plural or diminutive)

         k̓ʷétəŋ 'rat'--k̓ʷək̓ʷé?təŋ 'mouse' (vs. k̓ʷetəna·ɫ 'small
         rat (i.e. 'baby rat, rat offspring')

         sílə? 'grandparent'--səsílə? 'grandmother' (prob. 'granny')

         (skʷéčil 'day')--k̓ʷək̓ʷéyiɫ 'dawn'

         téŋəŋ 'getting night (8-9 p.m.)'--tətéŋəŋ 'evening (4-6 p.m.)'

C₁ə- + metathesis: skʷtá?́ 'raven'--skʷək̓ʷátə? 'crow'

-?-C₁V₁-: stáləw̓ 'river'--LD stá?taləw̓ (VU státaləw) 'creek'

         (VU,LD ŋə́ŋ stəɫtáləw̓ 'lots of rivers', VU,LD ŋə́ŋ stá?taləw̓
         'lots of creeks')

         poss. sáye? 'co-wife, husband of ex-wife, wife of ex-husband'
         --LD sə?áýsiye? 'two wives fighting'

C₁í-...-?-: ?--sƛíƛə̓ƛqəɫ (LD sƛíƛəƛqɫ) 'child' (suppletive pl.
         LD sté·x̌ʷəɫ, VU stéwix̌ʷəɫ 'children')

         stiqíw 'horse'--stitiqiw̓áɫɫ 'colt'

         other examples under 3.3.10

Notice that nominals are inflected with these affixes more than verbs are.

3.3.10. Combinations of aspect, plural and diminutive inflections.

old -C₁V₁C₂ (meaning unclear) (+ -lə- 'pl.'):

  sčé?če?--sčéləče? 'friends (esp. a crowd)'

C₁í- 'diminutive' (+ -?- 'continuative' + -lə- 'pl.'):

  šák̓ʷŋ 'bathe'--šišk̓ʷám 'swim'--šišk̓ʷá?am 'swimming'

  --LD šiləšk̓ʷám, VU šiləšk̓ʷə́m 'lots swimming'

C₁ə- 'continuative' (+ -əl- 'pl.'):

q̓ə́p 'gather'--q̓əlq̓ə́p 'a lot of people are gathering'

old C₁ə- (meaning unclear) (+ C₁í-...-ʔ- 'diminutive'):

LD x̣ʷəx̣ʷiẏə́qsn (VU final ṅ) 'he has a narrow nose'--LD
x̣ʷíʔx̣ʷəʔx̣ʷiẏ (VU x̣ʷix̣ʷəʔx̣ʷiẏ) 'thin (of rope, tree, etc.)'

C₁í-...-ʔ- 'diminutive' (+ -əl̓- 'pl.'):

LD pə́š ~ píš 'cat'--pəlíʔpəšpəš 'lots of kittens'

C₁ə- or -C₁ə- 'continuative' (+ -lə- or -əl- 'pl.'):

kʷələkʷəníṅət 'streetcar' (lit. 'lot of people running')

C₁ə- 'continuative' (+ -əl̓- 'pl.'):

sk̓ʷáθ̓ł (VU sk̓ʷác̓ł) 'crooked (tree, road, canoe, person)'
--sk̓ʷəlk̓ʷə́θ̓ (VU sk̓ʷəlk̓ʷə́c̓) 'real crooked'

p̓ə́ł 'to hatch'--p̓əlp̓ə́ł 'a lot hatched'

C₁ə- or -C₁ə- (meaning unclear) (+ -əl̓- 'pl.'):

sk̓ʷtáʔ 'raven'--sk̓ʷəlk̓ʷətáʔ 'lots of ravens'

C₁ə-...-ʔ-...metathesis 'diminutive' (+ -lə- or -əl- 'pl.'):

sk̓ʷək̓ʷáʔtəʔ 'crow'--sk̓ʷələk̓ʷáʔtəʔ 'lots of crows'

C₁ə- or -C₁ə- (meaning unclear) (+ -əl- 'pl.'):

nə́čŋ 'laughing'--nəlnəčátəṅ 'laughing over and over at
someone'

From these examples it appears that, except for the first example,
only C₁ə- or C₁í- reduplication types are attested co-occurring
with 'plural' and only l-infix plurals are attested with these
reduplication types; more data is needed to tell whether this
is accidental or a result of shifted or new types of affixation.

3.4. Nominals.

Nominals are noun-like words but often derived from verb roots, most often
with the s- 'nominalizer' prefix. (s- has an allomorph /š-/ before the
prefix x̣ʷ-; x̣ʷ- sometimes drops, leaving /š-/ as a portmanteau morpheme;
Montler 1984:45-48 glosses x̣ʷ- as 'locative' in Saanich but see 3.7 below.)
Some lexical affixes also seem to nominalize verbal roots in Samish:
čən- 'time for', nə- 'basic color' (may have more of a 'stative' flavor),
-tən ~ -ən 'device for, thing to'; some lexical affixes verbalize the
stem (most of which are verbal anyway); the remainder of lexical affixes
in the data gathered so far do not change syntactic classes.

Inflection of nominals includes possessive pronouns, plural, and diminutive
as already discussed and exemplified above. Derivational affixes are listed
in 3.7. Syntactically nominals are almost always preceded by demonstrative
articles (see 3.5) in nominal phrases which follow main or subordinate verbs.
Nominal phrases which are not co-referenced by pronoun affixes on the verb
are preceded by ʔə, called 'oblique case marker' by Thompson, Montler, and
others; this marker could also be analyzed as a prepositional verb (similar
to other such verbs); it is often translated by prepositions in English,

depending on remaining logical slots for the nominal phrase in the verb
phrase ('by' to show agent after a passive verb, 'to' or 'for' to show indirect
object after intransitive and some transitive verbs, etc., see text in
Chapter 5 below for many further examples and other prepositional translations).

The formation of relative clauses (any demonstrative article + verb)
and of subordinate clauses (demonstrative article kʷə + possessive pronoun
affix to show subject + s- or šxʷ- 'nominalizer' on the first verb of the
verb phrase to nominalize the whole phrase + verb phrase) strongly resembles
that of nominal phrases; as such they can be used in sentences as subjects,
objects, and oblique objects preceded by ʔə. It should be noted here that
the s- 'nominalizer' is often suffixed to the subordinating demonstrative
article kʷə or to the possessive pronoun attached to it (thus yielding
kʷs, kʷn̓s, kʷənəs); this is clear from aspirated allophones of stop-initial
words following--they would be unaspirated if the s- were prefixed; -s should
be written to produce the correct phonetic output. Indefinite nominals also
exist in Samish, usually (as in Upriver Halkomelem) based on interrogative verb
roots: ʔəw-mə́k̓ʷ-steŋ or ʔəw-mək̓ʷ-stéŋ 'everything', ʔəw̓ stéŋ ʔal̓
'anything', kʷə stéŋ ʔal̓ 'something' (as in LD,VU x̣č̓ə́tsxʷ kʷə stéŋ ʔal̓
'You figured something out.'), k̓ʷənélə 'how many people?, however many people,
a few people', kʷ sé?enəŋ ~ kʷ səns 'where(ver) one is at'. Usually indefi-
nites are nominalized with kʷə.

3.5. Demonstratives.

Samish demonstratives can be segmented for the most part into single-
consonant roots (specifying sex-gender and +/- invisibility/remoteness/
abstractness) and vowel-initial lexical suffixes (specifying distance from
the speaker). Some of these roots can co-occur in the same demonstrative
word. Demonstrative roots include:
kʷ 'invisible, remote; abstract; indefinite'
t 'not invisible, nor remote, nor abstract'
s 'female'
c 'male or gender unmarked'
(θ a rare variant for c, prob. phonological borrowing < Saanich/Halkomelem)
l ~ ʔ 'particular place' (ʔ allomorph only with //-éɫe//)
perhaps ɫ or ƛ̓ 'animate, gender unspecified'
Demonstrative suffixes include:
-ə 'unspecified distance, demonstrative article'
     (-ə is optionally dropped in allegro speech after kʷ and tɫ ~ ƛ̓)
-íyə 'proximate, near'
-éʔe 'non-proximate'
-əwlə ~ -əwləʔ 'distant, distal'
-éɫe ~ -éɫaʔ ~ -éɫəʔ 'proximate, near'
The final glottal stop on the last two suffixes may be an additional suffix
-ʔ 'emphasis' cognate with that found by Montler in Saanich.

Because nominal phrases must begin with a demonstrative article, articles
are most often translated by English 'the', 'a', etc. (kʷə also by 'some');
articles are also required before proper names and place names (where they
are not translated). Vocatives omit the article but are syntactically
unambiguous with verbs for two reasons: a) they are usually nominals
which are true nouns (like proper names or many kinterms), and b) they
occur sentence-initially followed only by particles preposed to a main
verb or by the main verb itself with no linking conjunction or subordinating
demonstrative article. Relative clauses and subordinate sentences must begin
with demonstrative articles too (the latter only with kʷə) (see 3.2, etc.
above).

Glosses of demonstratives (except for the sex-gender and near/not near/far
components) are more covertly present than overtly translated. The gender
distinctions however are often used contrastively with animate nominals
(few of which are inherently male or female). Thus ŋénəʔ 'offspring',
sʔéləxʷ 'parent', ʔíŋəs 'grandchild', sə nə ŋénəʔ 'my daughter',
sə sʔéləxʷ 'the mother', tə ʔíŋəs 'the grandson', etc. In fact,
other than third person independent pronouns (which use these same
demonstrative roots), demonstratives articles are the main means of
expressing sex-gender since verb subject and object affixes are ambiguous

as to gender. Demonstratives other than the articles are mainly verbal
in Samish (stative as in 'be here', adverbial as in 'here', or adjectival
as in 'this'--the three uses are distinguished by syntactic positions:
respectively in main/subordinate verb position, following or preceding
such a position (in apposition), and preceding a nominal while following
its article)(see text and paradigms for examples).

Found in Samish so far: kʷ ~ kʷə, kʷsə, (kʷθə?); tə, tíye, tə́wlə ~ tə́wlə?;
cə, (θə?), cé?e; tɬ ~ ƛ, ƛé?; sə (cf. səwníɬ); čsəlé?e,
kʷ sé?enəń; lé?e; ?éɬe ~ ?éɬa? ~ ?éɬə?, ?éɬe tiye ~? TB ?éɬti, če?éɬe.

Examples:
1. VU lá?a kʷ ?əẇ lé?e kʷ sésəẇ 'He's down at the beach.'
   TB kʷs šxʷqʷə́ltəns kʷə nəθélŋəxʷ 'the languages of different peoples'
   LD,VU háy kʷ sƛíƛəƛqɬ 'The child is finished.'
   LD,VU ?əẇ nə slə́l kʷə nə c̓sə́t 'I meant to hit him.'
   VU sk̓ʷéysə? kʷən skʷə́n·əxʷ kʷ s?íɬən čéɬe 'It will be impossible
   for you to get any food from here.'
   VU xʷəné́ŋs ?əl kʷ sčə́ɬ (LD šxʷəné́ŋs ?əl kʷ sčə́ɬ)(both xʷ prob. sic
   for x̣ʷ, and ?əl prob. sic for ?əi 'just') 'just any kind of wood'
   (x̣əné́ŋ 'kind of, similar to, like')
2. VU lé́ŋnəxʷ tə nə stíkʷən kʷsə nə stíkʷən 'My nephew saw my niece.'
   VU lé́ŋnəx kʷsə nə stíkʷən tə nə stíkʷən 'My niece saw my nephew.'
   VU ?éɬe yə́xʷ kʷƛi ?ené?e kʷsə siyém nə ŋənə? 'My dear daughter
   (not far but out of sight) must be coming here.'
3. TB ?əẇ txʷəhá·ysn čsəlé?e kʷθə ?əɬčéɬə? ?eɬtélŋəxʷ 'I'm the only one
   from those people way back.'
4. VU q̓pə́təs tə sɬnɬéniy tə sƛíƛəƛqəɬ 'The women are gathering the
      children.'
   LD,VU ?éɬa? tə sqʷəméẏ 'The dog is here.'
   LD,VU qʷə́ẏəx̣əń tə tə́ŋəxʷ 'the earth is shaking, earthquake'
5. VU níɬ kʷə tíye swə́ẏəqə? leŋətíɬtə 'This is the man we're watching.'
   VU tiẏe qéẏəs 'today'
   TB sƛí? kʷs x̣čínəxʷs tiye skʷé? nə šxʷqʷə́ltn 'He wants to learn this
   my own language.'
   TB ?əẇ txʷəhá·ysən ?əɬ ?éɬe tiye tə́ŋəxʷ 'I'm all alone on the land right
   here.'
   TB (citation form) ?éɬti 'here'
6. TB túlə nə́θe ~ túlə (//tə́wlə//) 'an other (= another?)'
   TB séməš nə čəléŋn lé?e təwlə? s?éməš 'My culture/background is
   Samish, that's over at Samish.'
   TB sə?étəŋsən kʷə yé? ?iq̓ə́nəsət ?ə tə́wlə qʷá? 'I was sent to go
   enter the water (over there).'
7. VU ?éwə kʷs níɬ sk̓ʷéy cə s?éməš 'The Samish never get hungry.'
   VU níɬsu kʷə́n·əxʷs cəw (//cə ?əẇ//) mə́kʷsəs sčéle?čəs tə s?íɬən líiəq

'And then all their many relatives got the food easily.'

VU x̣əɫásts ʔə cə ʔəw mək̓ʷstén sʔiɫən 'He's feeding them every kind of
food.'

VU léŋnəxʷs θə swə́ẏqə sə sɫenə́ẏ (LD léŋnəxʷs θə swəẏqəʔ θə sɫénəẏ)
'The man saw the woman.'

VU ƛ̓íẇsn kʷəʔʔə cəẇníɫ (LD ƛ̓íẇsn ʔə θəẇníɫ) 'I ran away from him.'
(vs. VU,LD ƛ̓íẇsn kʷəʔʔə səẇníɫ 'I ran away from her.')

VU leŋítəs cəw nəníʔɫiye 'She saw (visited) them.'

8. VU ʔəẇ níɫ kʷə céʔe swə́ẏqəʔ 'That's the man.'

VU níɫə céʔe sɫéni? 'Is that the woman?'

9. VU ʔéləŋ ətɫ spéˑs 'bear's house'

VU,LD xʷáŋəsxʷ ʔiʔq̓awétŋ ʔə ƛ̓əsə (or ƛ̓ ʔə́sə) 'Are you going to drum
for me?'

VU láʔa kʷə ʔəcéŋəstŋ ʔə ƛ̓ méli 'He was dressed by Mary.'

VU láʔa kʷə ʔəcéŋəstŋ ʔə ƛ̓ méli ʔə θə ʔíŋəs 'Mary dressed her grandson.'

10. VU,LD ƛ̓éʔ kʷəẇ sčéˑnəxʷ 'There's also fish.'

11. LD,VU sə nə stíkʷən 'my niece'

VU štéŋətəs sə sɫénəẏ 'He wished for the woman.'

VU nə sƛ̓íʔ kʷənə kʷánˑəxʷ sən ŋénə? 'I want to take your daughter.'

12. VU líləq ʔəl kʷs kʷánˑəxʷs tə sʔiɫən čsəléʔe kʷs ʔiʔəƛ̓íƛ̓əč
'It was just easy for them to get the food from down there at the bottom.'
(č— 'from', s— 'nominalizer' or 'stative')

TB nə šxʷčsəléˑ 'That's where I belong.'

13. VU kʷə séʔenəŋ 'where one is at' as in

VU wáʔačə (ʔ)əẇ kʷəṅs txʷənétəŋ kʷṅs yiʔáx̣ʷ ʔə kʷ séʔenəŋ sən sčéləʔče?
'I guess that's the way you're being taken when you're going where your
female relatives are at.'

14. VU láʔa kʷəẇ léʔe 'it's there'

VU tuʔ (//təẇ//) léʔe 'over there'

VU léʔe kʷə nə tén 'My mother is there.'
(vs. VU ʔéɫəʔ kʷə nə tén 'My mother is here.' [—ʔ perhaps 'emphatic'
because this sentence was elicited immediately after VU técəl kʷə nə tén
'My mother has got here.'])

VU láˑ kʷə léʔe kʷə nə tén 'My mother is way over there.'

VU níɫsu léʔesələʔ čéʔeys 'So that's where they were working.'

VU níɫsu léʔes cəẇ nəníʔɫiyeʔ ʔəɫtélŋəxʷ, sq̓épəɫ (~ sq̓əlq̓ép)
'So those people are there, gathered.'

15. VU kʷánˑəxʷəs tə sčéˑnəxʷ ʔəẇ stén ʔəl cəẇ mək̓ʷstén ƛ̓íƛ̓əč ʔéɫe
'They get fish, anything, everything on the sea-bottom right here.'

VU ʔn sƛ̓íʔ kʷsu ʔéɫes ʔə ɫníŋəɫ 'I want her here with us.'

16. TB kʷín ʔéɫe tíye téŋəxʷ 'born on this earth'
(also see above)

17. VU sƛ̓íʔs kʷs čtáləs ʔə sə sɫénəẏ čəʔéɫeʔ ʔə tə sq̓ʷíqʷəṅ 'He
wanted to get as a spouse a woman from here, out of the water.'

VU sk̓ʷéysəʔ kʷəṅ skʷánˑəxʷ kʷ sʔiɫən čéɫə kʷs yiƛ̓íƛ̓əč tə ʔəwmák̓ʷsteŋ

'It will be impossible for you to get any food from here, everything down
on the bottom.'

The Saanich system appears similar in general but differs in a number
of details from that of Samish.
   Saanich demonstratives have the following bases (Montler 1984):
-é?ə 'non-proximate', -í?ə 'proximate', -ə́wlə 'distant', -ə 'unspecified
   distance'
and the following initials:
kʷ- 'invisible, remote'
t- 'not invisible or generally extant'
ө- 'particular feminine individual'
s- 'particular individual, thing, or class'
l- 'particular place'
ł- 'particular near place'
lé?ə also is 'be at a particular place'
-? 'emphatic' can also be suffixed to any of these
those in -ə serve only as demonstrative articles
combinations found so far in Saanich include:
   kʷsə, kʷsé?ə, kʷsí?ə, kʷsə́wlə   rejected as demonstratives:
   kʷөə, kʷөé?ə, kʷөí?ə, kʷөə́wlə   *kʷə, *kʷí?ə, *tə, *té?ə, *tsə́wlə
   tsə, tsé?ə tí?ə, tə́wlə
   tlə, tlé?ə өlé?ə
   өə,   өé?ə, өí?ə, өə́wlə
         lé?ə
         łé?ə

3.6. Numerals.

   Samish, like other Straits dialects and most Salishan languages,
has lexical affixes which can be added to numerals and other word classes
and lexical affixes which can be added only to numerals. On numerals
both sets act like numeral classifiers, classifying following nominal
phrases or even allowing a class to be counted without a following nominal
phrase. A few of these have been elicited but so far no concerted effort
has been made to elicit complete sets or the full range of classifier
affixes in Samish. For Sooke, Efrat 1969:137-141 gives affixes which
classify: diminutive, collective, number of times, pieces/bunches/packages,
people, dollars/round objects, days, day of the week, tribe/people,
buildings/houses/stores, multiples of ten, and canoes. For Upriver
Halkomelem, Galloway 1977:422-427 reports affixes for dollars, people,
o'clock, day of the week, paddles/paddlers, times, fish, multiples of ten,
trees, piles, garments, houses, canoes, pants, spherical objects/fruit,
containers, young, wives, poles/uprights, and possibly birds. Samish
numerals, unless placed in clause/sentence-initial verb position,

normally are preceded by demonstrative articles and function as nominals
or as adjectives preceding the nominals.
Thus: VU ?ə̓w̓ ni⁺ə kʷə čé?sə? 'Is that those two people?'
 VU ⁺éləč ?ə tə néc̓a? q̓éləŋs 'He's blind in one eye.'
 VU ?ápən ?i kʷə čə́sə s?ə⁺ténəŋ 'There's twelve berries.'

   It is not clear yet which classifiers are obligatory in Samish (though
those for 'people' and 'day of the week' seem to be); nominals for which
there are no classifiers or for which classifiers are optional can be
counted by the unclassified numerals (see below).

   Samish numerals 'one' to 'four' appear unanalyzable; 'five', 'six',
'eight', 'twenty', and further multiples of ten (including '100') are
analyzable (see below). Numbers between multiples of ten are constructed
additively, i.e. 'eleven' is literally "ten and a one" (Welk ca 1950).
'Thousand' is borrowed from English; multiples of hundred (and thousand)
are constructed on the model of: multiple + hundred/thousand, i.e. '200'
is VU néc̓a? snéc̓əwəč.

   Samish has the following unclassified numerals (VU unless noted):
VU néc̓a?, LD,TB néθ̓ə 'one'
VU čə́sa? ~ čə́sə?, LD,TB čə́se? 'two'
VU,LD,TB ⁺íxʷ 'three'
VU,LD,TB ŋás 'four'
VU ⁺q̓áycəs (á ~ ə́ ~ é), LD ⁺q̓éycəs, TB ⁺q̓écəs 'five' (cf. ⁺q̓ə́t 'wide',
  -səs ~ -čəs 'hand')
VU,LD,TB t̓x̣ə́ŋ 'six' (cf. √tx̣ in VU t̓[-ə⁺-]t̓x̣-ə́sət tə stáləw̓ 'the river
  forks')
VU c̓ákʷəs, LD θ̓ákʷs, TB θ̓ákʷəs 'seven'
VU té?səs, TB té?(e)səs, LD té?s· 'eight' (cf. -səs 'hand')
VU təkʷəx̣ʷ, VU,TB tə́kʷəx̣ʷ, LD tə́kʷx̣ʷ 'nine'
VU,LD,TB ?ápən 'ten'
?ápən ?i kʷ néc̓a? 'eleven'
VU c̓əx̣ʷk̓ʷə́s (c̓ ~ θ̓), TB,LD θ̓əx̣ʷk̓ʷə́s 'twenty' (cf. k̓ʷs-ə́ŋ 'to count'?)
VU,LD θ̓əx̣ʷk̓ʷə́s ?í kʷ ⁺íxʷ 'twenty-three'
⁺ə́x̣ʷə⁺šé? 'thirty'
ŋəs⁺še? 'forty'
⁺q̓ə́čə⁺še? 'fifty'
t̓x̣ə́mə⁺še? 'sixty'
θ̓ə́kʷə⁺šè? 'seventy' (θ̓ ~ c̓)
téčə⁺šè? 'eighty'
tə́kʷəx̣ʷše? 'ninety'
VU. néc̓əwəč ~ néc̓e snéc̓əwəč, LD néθ̓ə néc̓əwəč, TB néθ̓e snéc̓əwəč 'one
  hundred' (cf. néc̓ 'different', -əwəč 'on the bottom, rump'?)
čə́sə snéc̓əwəč 'two hundred'

néča? téwsən   'one thousand'
VU,LD,TB ŋə́n 'many, much, lots of'
k̓ʷín 'how many?, how much?'

Classified numerals:
VU k̓ʷənélə 'how many persons?, a few people'
VU,LD k̓ʷək̓ʷənél̓a? 'just a few people (three or so)'
VU nənéwəčə? 'one person'
VU čé?sə? 'two people'
VU,LD səŋé 'twice' (note suppletive root)
VU səŋnét or siŋnét ([sɪŋnét]) 'Monday' (lit. "second day")
 (cf. VU sx̣e?x̣əl̓nét 'Sunday' (lit. "holy/forbidden day"), VU čəlqʷl̓nét
 'Tuesday' (√čəlqʷ possibly 'fall, drop', -l̓nét 'day, night'))
VU sl̓íxʷs 'Wednesday' (s-...-s circumfix?, root 'three')
VU sŋás 'Thursday' (s-...-s circumfix?, root 'four')
VU sl̓q̓éyčəs 'Friday' (s-...-s circumfix?, root 'five')('Saturday' is
 q̓ə́mətəŋ, lit. "it was purposely cut in half", cf. q̓ə́m 'cut in half')
VU snáθ̓ə? 'spouse (slang), (my) other half' (θ̓ ~ č̓)

3.7. Lexical Affixes.

    Lexical affixes in Samish are for the most part derivational or
incorporative. They usually add quite concrete lexical meanings.
A large group of them are somatic or body-part suffixes; these are
locative in nature, locating the action on a body part or being done
with or to a body part; some also have figurative extensions to
geography as in English "a neck of land", etc. The following list
is bound to be incomplete but includes all Samish lexical affixes
I have been able to isolate to date (from all the data but the texts).

=éˑn, =éˑn̓, =éʔen 'angular, (flat-pointed)'
=imaʔ, LD =íˑmaʔ, VU =íˑməʔ 'appearance, in appearance'
=əl=éχən, =əl=éχən̓, =əl̓=éχən̓, =éχən, =əχən 'arm, wing, side of
  rigid object (fence, house), part of house'
=áɫ(=)ən 'on the back (or spine?)'?
=ič, =íč, =əwéč, =éwəč 'on the back/spine, at the back' (sometimes
  merges in shape and meaning with suffix for 'bottom')
=sət 'become, get (inceptive)'
=əʔ 'being, person'?
=ŋəxʷ, =él=ŋəxʷ, =əl̓=ŋəxʷ 'being, living thing, person'?
=íqən, =íqən̓ 'belly'
=ámaʔ, =áˑmaʔ 'berry'
poss. =əyí 'big'?
=íws, =íw̓s, =íkʷəs, =ikʷs, =íkʷə (_-t), =əkʷəs, =ə́ws, =ə́w̓s 'in the
  body, on the body, skin, on the surface'
=(ə́)weč, =əwéč, =əw̓éč, =áw̓əč, =ə́wəč, =əw̓əč, =eč, =əč 'on the bottom,
  on the rump, on the tail, at the bottom (geog.), in the bottom'
=nəč 'on the bottom, tail'
=íp, =əp 'on the bottom'
=éˑlŋəxʷ, VU =élŋəxʷ, LD =élənəxʷ 'breast, milk, in the breast, in the
  milk'
VU =(h)éwtxʷ ~ =(ʔ)éwtxʷ ~ =éw̓txʷ, LD =(h/ʔ)éwxʷ ~ =(h/ʔ)éw̓xʷ 'building,
  house'
=əwəɫ, =əw̓əɫ (LD =əw̓ɫ)(poss. < Halkomelem), =wəɫ, =(w)əɫ, =áˑɫ 'canoe'
=ínəs 'in the chest'
=áˑɫ (once ~ =á(ʔ)aɫ), =əɫ, =áy̓ɫ, =eɫ (poss. =əyɫ), =əčɫ, =álɫ (prob.
  < Halkomelem) 'child, offspring, baby, young'
=əl=íčən, =əl=éčən, =éčən, =əy̓čən, =əčən 'circumference, on the waist,
  around the waist/arm/wrist'
=əl̓kʷət 'clothes'
nə= 'basic color'
=élə, =(h)élə 'contains, container of, place for'
=iy̓, =éy̓, =əy̓, =iʔ 'covering, bark, wood, cedar bark'
s=...=s, =əs 'day of the week, day, cyclic period'

=ɬnét, =nét   'day, night'

=é·ɬ, =əɬ   'deceased'

q=...=éləɬ ~ q=...=é·ɬ   'deceased'

=áy̓e, =áy̓ə, =iye?, =əye?   'diminutive, a little; female name ending'

=ánəp   'dirt, earth'

=kʷí·l(a?)   'dishes, inside of canoe'

=əné?, =ənə, =ən̓   'in the ear, on the ear, on the side of the head'

=á?s   'edge'

=əl̓=íwə?   'fish eggs'?

=(h)áləs, =áləs   'on the eyes, around the eye, color, in color, looks
   like'

=á·s, =ás, =as, =əs   'on the face, in the face, face (of an object)',
   =ás=əŋ   'around, directionless',
   =iy=ás   'around, in a circle'

=ál̓=əče?   'on the fingers, on the hand?'

=əw̓sə?, =əw̓sə?, =əw̓sə, =əw̓s   'fire',
   =(ál=)əw̓sə? (LD =ál=əw̓s(ə))   'firewood'

=ečəp   'fire'

=šən, =šən, =šən̓, =šə (_tən), =sən ~ =sən̓   'in/on the foot and leg,
   on the foot, on the leg' (see also under 'precipitation')

tən̓=   'from'

=il̓, =il̓, =il, =əl̓, =əl   'go, come, become, get, inceptive, -ish'

=ənəkʷ   'ground'

=ánəq   'habitual'

=čis ~ =čəs, =sis (?), =səs, =ésəs (LD =és·)   'hand, in the hand, on
   the finger'

č=   'to have, produce'

=əl=í?qʷ, =əl=íqʷ, =í?qʷ, =íqʷ, =əqʷ   'on the head, on top of the head,
   on the hair of the head, hair',
   =a?qʷ, =áw̓əqʷ   'hat'
   poss. =əqʷ, =iyəqʷ, =ayəqʷ   gloss uncertain but appears in the
    words for 'great grandparent/–child', 'great great grandparent/–child',
    and 'great great great grandparent/–child' (root meanings unclear)

=qən, =qən̓   'inside the head, in the head' (poss. related to 'in the
   throat' see below)

=ək̓ʷ   'head gristle'

=əqʷ   'hole' ('dig' < 'make hole')

=íwən (LD =íwən̓), =íkʷən   'on the inside, on the insides'

=əp̓, =p̓   'on itself'

=éɬse, =éɬsə, =áɬs   'unclear liquid'

=əl(=)nəq   'sibling's man'? (combines with root meaning 'different' to
   produce 'wife's sister's husband'; could be related to =əq 'penis, male')

təx̌ʷ=, tax̌ʷ=   'mid-'

=éw̓ən̓, =íkʷən, =əkʷən   'in the mind, thoughts, feelings'

?i?=, ?i=, yi=   'in motion, while moving'

=ásən, =əsən   'in the mouth, mouth (of river)',
   =áysən, =áysə (_tən)   'in the mouth, lip, jaw, chin'
txʷ=   'mutative (gradual change of state)'
=əɫwət, =əlwət   'female name ending' (see 'clothing' suffix)
=á·t (=əmá·t, =sá·t, =əlá·t, =əwá·t)   'female name ending'
=əye?   'female name ending' (see 'diminutive' suffix above)
=(t)əq   'male name ending' (see 'male, penis' ending below)
=əlénəxʷ, =énəxʷ   'male name ending'
=íləm   'male name ending'
=ímət   'male name ending'
=tən   'male name ending' (see 'thing made to' suffix below)
=əltxʷ   'male name ending'
=éčsŋ   'on the back of the neck and head'
š=   'nominalizer, thing, device'
š=xʷ=   'nominalizer, device for' (minimal contrast: š=xʷ=ʔíɫən   'dish,
   plate', s-ʔíɫən 'food', ʔíɫən 'to eat a meal')
(s-   'nominalizer', more grammatical than lexical)
=él=əqsən, =éqsən, =əqsən, =qsən, =qs   'on the nose/point/end, in the nose,
   point (geog.), bill (of bird)'
poss. =VₗCₗ   'out-of-control' (in 'stutter')
=əl=kʷəs, LD =əɫ=kʷəs   'paddle'
=émən̓, =éŋən̓   'part of'
=əq   'penis, male, on the pubic area'
=él=ŋəxʷ, =él=nəxʷ, =l=ŋəxʷ, =ŋəxʷ, (=məxʷ prob. < Halkomelem)   'people,
   tribe, person' (the -l- element could be a pluralizer here)
=éla?, =elə   'persons' (numeral classifier)
=šən, =šn̓, =sən   'precipitation' (see also 'leg/foot' suffix)
=éɫe   'proximate (here)'
=é?e   'non-proximate (there)'
=íŋ   'repeatedly'
=áɫs, =áls   'round thing, rock, fruit'
=éləẃəɫ, =əlwəɫ, =(é)ẃəɫ, =kʷíɫ, =kʷəɫ   'on the side, side (of body,
   of other things, disposition of a person), dimension'
poss. =əɫqəy̓   'snake' (in sínəɫqəy̓ 'giant supernatural lizard-like creature
   that lives in lakes (if one sees it and tells one spits blood and dies)'
   and in ʔéɫqəy̓ 'snake')
poss. =éləqɫ   'sound'?
=álkʷɫ   'spirit power'
=é?ɫ   'stature'
=éys   'stockings/leggings'? (may be related to 'covering' suffix)
=ém   'strength'
=á·ɫ, =əɫ   '-style, -kind, -type, belongs to, -ish'
=émən̓, =émən   'taste'
=tən   'thing, device, thing to, device for, something that, made for'
   ('made for' is prob. the best translation for this since it does not

necessarily nominalize; many words with =tən also have s- or š-xʷ=
nominalizers too)

=ən   'thing made to, thing to/for, device to/for'

=nə   '-thing, -body' (follows negative verb ʔə́wə 'no, have no, be no')

=ə́qən, =qén, =qən̓   'in the throat, in voice, speech, language, sound'

=ɬnəɬ   'in the gullet, inside the throat'

čn̓=   'time, season'

=əɬ=šéʔ   'times ten' (=šéʔ prob. is 'ten' here since Saanich has =éɬ,
as does Halkomelem, for 'times' as a numeral classifier yielding ordinals
with 'three' and several succeeding numbers; ordinals have not yet been
elicited for Samish but surely exist)

=(í)xʷsəɬ   'tongue'

=ə́nəs   'on the teeth, tooth'

=íɬč, =éɬč, =iɬč, =əɬč   'tree, plant'

=əɬp   'tree, plant' (in loans < Halkomelem)

prob. =əč̓ 'twist'?

=əš   'upright'

t̓əi̓=   'variable'?

=éi̓ŋən̓ (LD =éi̓əŋən̓)   'want to'

=éləq, =əléʔq, =əléq, =léq, =ələq   'wave'

=éi̓qən, =éi̓qən, =ə́i̓qən̓, =éi̓qən, =ələqən   'wool, soft covering, hair'

xʷ=   gloss uncertain, prob. not 'locative' with somatic affixes since these
are locative without xʷ=; appears in tribal names, with 'open it up',
'lock it', 'it closed on its own', 'generous', 'cougar', 'hit someone in
the face', 'patch it'

=əyéč, =əyíč, =iy̓(=)əč, poss. =iyáč   gloss uncertain, could be two
suffixes, =əy̓ 'covering' plus =íč 'on the back'; appears with
'overflowing from being piled up' and 'piled up' (√'burst?'),
perhaps in 'grasshopper' (√'jumping'), and '(unidentified plant,
perhaps wild onion)' (√q̓ʷəxʷ gloss uncertain)

I regret there is no time to cite examples for each of these affixes
here. Examples can be found in the word list below and in examples given
above. The connective element =él= ~ =éi̓= ~ =əl= ~ =əi̓= may serve
or may have served some function or added some lexical meaning but which
is unclear so far; other connectives such as those beginning in =a
appear to add lexical meanings, but it is unclear whether they will turn
out to be consistent. Further study is also required to define environments which determine the occurrence of the allomorphs given for each
affix; some are clearly phonologically predictable, some are lexically
determined, and some are a mixture (Montler 1984 makes a good start on
such prediction for the Saanich lexical affixes).

3.8. Particles.

Samish particles cover a wide range of tense, mood, modal, and
adverbial categories. The main characteristic they share is that
they cannot be inflected. Saanich particles given by Montler 1984 include
proclitics:
kʷɬ 'realized ('already' + situations where 'already' is inappropriate in
English)', s 'unrealized' (ʔə́wə, xʷəwé _ subord. cl.)(_ ʔəẃ,ʔiʔ),
ʔiʔ 'accompanying' ('moving with' (my gloss) and 'and'), ʔəẇ 'contempora-
neous' ('contrastive to preceding info.' (sums up Montler's explanation)),
čəɬ 'immediate past', təwə 'still, yet', ʔiʔwəwə 'perhaps, maybe';
and enclitics:
ə 'yes/no question', čə 'command', čəʔ 'evidential',
yəq 'optative' (usu. transl. 'I wish, I hope, I ought' even if subj. is
not 1st person, 'ought' appears with 'past' ləʔ), yəxʷ 'conjectural'
(usu. transl. 'must be (not obligation/necessity)'), q 'conditional' (too
rare to say much, 1 ex. after háʔ 'if, when'), ləʔ 'past', səʔ 'future',
person markers sən/ɬtə/sxʷ, q̇əʔ 'emphatic', kʷəʔ 'informative' (poss.
'new information' for example a sentence without is used "if you're asking me"
but sentence with kʷəʔ used "if I'm telling you"), ʔačə 'request information'
(not used with ə but with question words for 'what', 'who', 'whose',
'when', 'where' where the speaker sincerely doesn't know the answer
—txʷ-sén 'whose?', sén 'who is it?', ʔəx̣ín 'where is it?', txʷ-ʔəx̣ín
'where is s-o going?', s-tén 'what is it?', ʔín̓-ət 'what did s-o say/mean?'),
kʷəčə 'explanative' (offer of or request for info., in requests it appears
with ʔə, xʷənín̓/x̣ʷənín̓ 'how?, why?'), helə '2nd person pluralizer',
ʔaɬ 'limiting' (usu. 'just, only, merely'), čtəʔ 'probable', waʔačə
'presumptive' (usu. 'I guess');
also demonstratives;
ʔə 'oblique case marker';
and kʷə 'subordinator'.
These are in the following position classes:

preposed or proclitic				postposed or enclitic				
ʔə	kʷɬ	ʔiʔ	čəɬ	ə	čəʔ	ləʔ	sən	q̇əʔ
kʷə	s	ʔəẇ	təwə	čə	yəq	səʔ	ɬtə	kʷəʔ
		ʔiʔwəwə ?		yəxʷ			sxʷ	ʔačə
				q				kʷəčə
								helə
								ʔaɬ

čtə ?
waʔačə ?

(question marks mean position unknown within proclitic or enclitic groups)

The Samish particles found so far include demonstratives(3.5) and:

preposed or proclitic			postposed or enclitic			
ʔə	kʷɬ	ʔiʔ(-)	-ə	yəxʷ,yuw	(-)sən	səʔ,saʔ

```
Preposed                                    postposed
kʷə    s-    (ʔ)əw̓  tuwəʔ,tuw̓,təw̓     čə  saʔ,səʔ   (-)ɬtə    kʷəʔ
(láʔa, LD luw̓,ləw̓,luw)                         (-)sxʷ    (h)elə
         ʔiwáwaʔ ʔ                                       kʷəčə,skʷəče
                                                         ʔaɬ    ʔəčə,ʔəče
                              wáʔačə,TB wá·č ʔ
```

Notice several differences in position from Saanich. láʔa (LD luw̓, etc.)
is not enclitic in Samish but is used as an auxiliary verb and takes the
pronoun subject inflections normally found on the main verb; what English
translates as the main verb is then subordinated after kʷə and any of the
phrase's proclitics. The other Samish 'past' tense is so far only attested
as a suffix and so is omitted here. ʔiʔ 'accompanying' in Samish is sometimes
prefixed (as ʔiʔ- ~ ʔi- ~ yi-, usually the latter) when meaning 'in motion,
in transition'; when meaning 'and' it takes the form ʔiʔ ~ ʔi and functions
as a simple conjunction (both of numerals, nominal phrases, verb phrases,
and whole sentences). I have not found any examples yet of čəɬ 'immediate
past', but it may well occur in yet untranscribed texts of LD or conversations.
The same is true for the Samish cognates with Saanich čə 'command', yəq
'optative', q 'conditional', q̓əʔ 'emphatic', and čtə 'probable': no examples
in Samish yet.

   Samish s- 'unrealized' is phonologically prefixed (usually to (ʔ)əw̓
'contrastive');   it sometimes coalesces phonologically with the
subordinating demonstrative kʷə to yield kʷsəw̓ ~ kʷsu. It is often
translated in texts as 'so' or 'then'. More examples of negatives in
Samish are needed to tell whether this s- functions there as in Saanich.
Samish -ə 'yes/no question' is phonologically a suffix in all but one
or two examples (there it is ʔə, an enclitic, homophonous with ʔə 'oblique
case marker'). Samish čə 'evidential' is attested preceding yəxʷ 'conjectural (must be)' and so is in a different position class than its
Saanich cognate čəʔ. Samish saʔ ~ səʔ 'future' has not been attested yet
following yəxʷ, so I have not listed them in separate positions as in
Saanich. Samish saʔ ~ səʔ however is attested both before and after the
subject pronoun position class. The subject pronouns (-)sən, (-)ɬtə,
and (-)sxʷ are more often phonologically suffixed than postposed but do
occur both ways. Samish kʷəčə '(explanative?)' is found once after səʔ
'future' but elsewhere appears as skʷəče. Samish ʔəčə ~ ʔəče '(request
information?)' occurs once after ʔaɬ 'just, simply, merely' and so in
Samish must be in a position class after that containing ʔaɬ. There
are a few other minor differences between Samish and Saanich particles
in form (Samish ʔaɬ ~ ʔal ~ ʔəɬ ~ ʔəl are not shown on the table).
Functions and translations of the Samish particles are very much the
same as those given for Saanich by Montler 1984.
   There is one additional class of words within Samish particles,
interjections. So far only a few have been found: hé·ʔe 'yes', ʔənəné
'(said if scared)', ʔa 'oh' (as in VU ʔá siýém̓ 'oh respected person

(used when talking to a person and especially when encouraging a public speaker)', ʔečənə́(ʔ) 'gee, oh my gosh!', and possibly ʔəš̌á:ːʔ '(said if one sees something he hardly ever sees)' (this last may be Cowichan or the same in both Cowichan and Samish). There are quite likely more (Galloway 1977 lists 16 or so, including cognates with all of those shown here).

4. CLASSIFIED WORD LIST FOR SAMISH

4.0. Introduction.

This word list approximately follows the classified word list developed
by Aert Kuipers and Randy Bouchard for Amerindian languages of the Pacific
Northwest. The nominals are listed by semantic domains, adjectival and
adverbial verbs are listed by pairs of antonyms, and verbs are listed in
alphabetic order by English gloss. I have expanded most sections but not
that on verbs; verbs listed are mainly those quoted in earlier sections of
the present work. A listing by semantic domain also would properly list all
the verbs, classified numerals, lexical affixes, and adjectives and adverbs
appropriate under each semantic domain, not just nominals. I have tried
to do this to some extent but more could be done. This word list makes
no attempt at being a dictionary; for that a better organization would
be alphabetic by Samish with an English finder list. I regret there is
no time to even try that organization on the present incomplete list.
The present list has been entered on a computer and with additions and
massive reorganization may serve as the kernel of a dictionary in several
years. Forms given below are by both VU and LD unless noted; where forms
by TB are identical they are shown by (=TB).

4.1. Word List.

Numerals (also see 3.6)
   one   VU nə́c̓ə?, LD,TB nə́θə
   two   VU č̓ə́sa? ~ č̓ə́sə?, LD,TB č̓ə́se?
   three   VU,LD,TB ƛ́íxʷ
   four   VU,LD,TB ŋás
   five   VU ƛ̓q̓áyč̓əs (á ~ ə́ ~ é), LD ƛ̓q̓éyč̓əs, TB ƛ̓q̓éč̓əs
   six   VU,LD,TB t̓x̌ə́ŋ
   seven   VU c̓ák̓ʷəs, LD θ̓ák̓ʷs, TB θ̓ák̓ʷəs
   eight   VU té?səs, TB té?(e)səs, LD té?s·
   nine   VU tə́kʷəx̌ʷ, VU,TB tə́kʷəx̌ʷ, LD tə́kʷxʷ
    ten   VU,LD,TB ?ápən
   eleven   VU ?ápən ?i kʷ nə́c̓ə?
   twenty   VU c̓əxʷk̓ʷə́s (c̓ ~ θ̓), LD,TB θ̓əxʷk̓ʷə́s
   twenty-three   θ̓əxʷk̓ʷə́s ?í kʷ ƛ́íxʷ
   thirty   VU ƛ́əxʷəƛšé?
   forty   VU ŋásƛšè?
   fifty   VU ƛ̓q̓éč̓əƛšè?
   sixty   VU t̓x̌ə́məƛšè?
   seventy   VU θ̓ə́kʷəƛšè?
   eighty   VU téč̓əƛšè?
   ninety   VU tə́kʷəx̌ʷšé?

one hundred VU néčəwəč ~ náče snéčəwəč, LD nə́θə néčəwəč,
 TB nə́θe snéčəwəč
two hundred VU čə́sə snéčəwəč
one thousand VU nə́čaʔ téwsən
many, much, lots of VU,LD,TB ŋə́ṅ
how many?, how much? VU k̓wín
how many people?, a few people VU k̓wənéla
just a few people (three or so) k̓wək̓wəṅéla?
one person VU nənéwəc̓ə?
two people VU čéʔsə?
twice səŋé

Nature (inanimate features, weather)
    the whole world šq̓wáq̓wəqsn
    land téŋəxw (=TB)
    earthquake, the earth is shaking q̓wə́y̓əx̣əṅ tə téŋəxw
    mountain, rock VU sŋénət, LD,TB sŋé·nt

cliff VU síɫəs
sidehill VU xwsíɫəs, LD xwsíɫs
cleft or crack in rock face ("cracked") VU séq̓əɫ
field, grassy clearing (for ex. on island) spéɫx̣ən ~ spə́ɫx̣ən
woods VU šéšič ~ šíšič
on top of the mountain VU scéc̓ə ʔə tə sŋénət
a rockslide happened číqəŋ tə sŋénət
a snowslide happened číqəŋ tə ŋéqə?
wind spxwéla?, spxwél·a?, VU sčáŋ
wind when its snowing, north wind sčáy̓əm
warm wind, east wind stíwət
south wind VU sqéṅət, LD sqéṅət
west wind sčáɫəqw
wind from the west tṅčáɫəqw
good calm (of water or wind) ʔə́y̓ slíqwəl
moon ɫqé·ic̓
star VU,TB kwásən
sky VU səsítən, LD səsítəṅ, TB sísəɫ (= 'high, up, above')
cloud VU ʔesítŋ
there's a lot of puffy clouds (as before a rain) VU məlmə́qwsət tə ʔesítŋ
cloudy on a bad day šṅə́w̓əs
thunder, thunderbird sxwəxwáʔas ~ sxwəxwáʔas
have a thunderstorm q̓wə́y̓əx̣sət tə sxwəxwáʔas ("thunderbird is shaking
    himself")
lightning ("thunderbird is opening his eyes") k̓wəléc̓il tə sxwəxwáʔas
lightning on land ("the land is burning") čə́qw tə téŋəxw
lightning flashes in the sky ("the sky is burning") čə́qw tə səsítən

the northern lights čákʷəł tə səsítəⁿ (kʷ poss. qʷ?)

to rain ƚə́məxʷ (=TB)

to stop raining VU xʷécsən ~ xʷéɵsən

to hail, hailing qəmélšⁿ

between snow and rain and hail ƚəlqəmélšəⁿ

ice síma?, s·íma? (=TB)

frost χéχəⁿ

snow on the ground ŋéqə?, TB ŋéqe?

snow falls in the air číq

frozen səsíma?

  freeze TB símatŋ ~ símatŋ

dew sá?sχʷ

rainbow xʷə́ƚašən

water qʷá?

fresh water χáẇəs qʷá?

sea, salt water ƚƚéƚsə, ƚéƚⁿ qʷá?, TB ƚƚéƚɵə

spring water mətáqʷəŋ qʷá?

river stáɬəẇ (=TB)

  small creek VU státaləẇ, LD stá?taləẇ

lake χáčə?, TB χáče

  small lake χəχá?če?

dam across river VU stə́q, LD štə́q (√təq 'closed')

pool šxʷ?í?ič ~ šxʷ?í·č

wave sqʷƚəlé?qən

bottom of water ƚéčƚ

clear water xʷ?ə́ẏəⁿ qʷá?

muddy water xʷŋíxʷəł qʷá?

whirlpool, twisting water sχə́ləč qʷá?

whirlwind q̇ʷəl̇q̇ʷə́ł̇šⁿ

upstream téẏit, tətéyət

downstream VU wáq̇ʷəł, LD wáq̇ʷł

tide moving (either in or out) VU xʷəŋéləqən

tide comes in (for ex. viewed from shore) qə́məl

tide is coming in (for ex. viewed from sea) VU qéməl̇

tide is already in VU qəmqə́məl

tide goes out šém

tide is out VU šémšm

high tide, water up high VU q̇éŋq̇əŋe?

low tide, water goes down VU ?i šéšəm

half tide, half water VU stáq̇ʷəł qʷá?

low wave ƚíxʷənən

high wave VU sqʷléqŋ

foam in the water (like in a boat's wake) ?əyáməl(əč) ?

beach, shore; down at the beach VU sésəẇ

going along a shore in a canoe ?isčəlíqʷ

bay   VU šŋéʔčəč

coming out of a bay   VU səqəlíč ~ sqəlíč, LD sqəlíčəŋ

a point of land   VU sʔíləqs

going around a point   sʔíləqsŋ

inlet, mouth of a river   VU nəwəlíč

coming into the mouth of a river   nəwəlíčŋ

drop-off in water   sxʷíyəqən

tiny island   LD suxʷíqʷ

big island   LD s(xʷ)qʷíseʔč ??

island connected to mainland and sometimes cut off by tide   VU ćíxʷən

steep rock drop-off (on island for ex.)   VU hílən sŋénət

snag   VU x̣əẏəmnəč

driftwood   VU sčiyáyəɫ

smooth black shiny rock used for arrowheads and by new spirit dancers
    (found on beaches)(prob. obsidian)   k̉əńtáls ("porpoise rock")

sand; sandbar   pqʷéčən (=TB)

gravel, pebbles   VU ċx̣ét, LD θ̣x̣ét

dust or smoke is spreading, dust is flying   VU pék̉ʷəŋ

steam   spáləxʷŋ

steam rising (like from moss in morning sun or water on a fire)
    VU pəláxʷŋ̉

fog   VU,TB spéʔxʷəŋ

foam   VU spáq̉ʷəŋ

a drop of water   VU sćqəŋ

slow dripping   VU ćéq̉əŋ

clay   VU séyəq̉

(soft) mud   VU ƛ̉əkʷƛ̉əkʷ

wet ground from spring or dripping water   VU ćíq̉əɫ ~ θ̣íq̉əɫ

iron   qəmtən

gold   kúl ~VU kʷú·l

poison   VU ćéx̣tən

dawn (light just before sun rises)   VU kʷəkʷéyiɫ

sunrise, the sun just showed   VU kʷíɫ tə sqʷəqʷéɫ

early in morning (after sun's up, 6 or 7 am)   VU kʷəćíɫ

to be day   VU kʷéčil

  a day   skʷéčil (=TB)

hot day   q̉éləs skʷéčil (q̉ʷ ~ k̉ʷ)

cold day   VU ćáʔɫəŋ skʷéčil, LD θ̣áʔɫəŋ skʷéčil

noon   VU təx̣ʷq̉élət

evening (5-6 pm)   VU tətéŋəŋ̉

getting dark (inside house, or eyes, or dusk)   VU ɫéčsət

getting night (8-9 pm)   VU téŋəŋ̉

night   VU snét, TB nét

midnight   VU təx̣ʷnét

today   VU tiẏe qéẏəs

yesterday VU čəléqɬ (or čiléqɬ)

day before yesterday VU txʷə́nəɬnét ("day on the other side")

tomorrow VU kʷəkʷéčələs

day after tomorrow VU qəqəɫétəs skʷéčil, VU qəɫét kʷéčil

springtime VU q̓ə́q̓ʷəlás ~ yiq̓ʷíwələs, LD hiʔq̓ʷíwələs

summer VU q̓ʷé·ləs ~ VU,LD čṅkʷéləs

autumn VU c̓ɫáṅsət ("gets cold"), LD hiʔə̓ɫáṅst

wintertime LD čṅə̓áɬṅ

fire VU sčəqʷə́w̓səʔ ~ sčəqʷúʔsəʔ

firewood VU sčáɬ

kindling VU čéčx̣ (poss. číčx̣)

sparking VU ƛ̓lqʷéls

a fire (flames) VU sə́nəw̓səʔ

to burn čə́qʷ (=TB)

smoke is spreading, to smoke VU p̓áƛ̓ən

smoke all over (from grass burning) VU sp̓áləƛ̓ṅ

smoke coming out, smoking VU p̓əláƛ̓ṅ

go out (of a fire) VU ƛ̓ə́kʷ

  put out a fire ƛ̓ə́k̓ʷəlaʔ

ashes VU q̓ʷéy̓ečəp (é ~ ə́), LD q̓ʷéʔečp

black ashes, charcoal VU číčət, LD číə̓t

Fauna

animal TB tsá·lṅəxʷ, VU tsálṅəxʷ, LD tətásəlṅəxʷ (prob. 'small animal')

bear (any kind) VU spéʔes

  bear cub VU speʔesá·ɬ

deer, (deer) meat smáyis ~ smə́yis, TB smáyiθ

  white-tailed deer VU p̓q̓ə́wəč smáyis

  buck VU swə́y̓qəʔ smə́yis ("male deer") ~ c̓ístn smə́yis ("antler deer")

  doe VU sɫéni̓ʔ smə́yis

mountain goat VU p̓q̓ə́lqən ("white wool")

elk VU q̓ayé·č

moose poss. kʷíwič ~ kʷíwəy̓č (same as in Cowichan)

horse VU stiqíw

wolf VU stq̓ə́yeʔ

dog VU sqʷəmə́y̓, TB sqʷəméy

  puppy sqʷəmey̓á·ɬ

mink VU čəči̓ʔqən, LD čečíqən (VU defers to this form)

beaver VU sqəléw̓

porcupine LD ə̓əlčə́lqən (č prob. ə̓ also)

raccoon VU (s)x̣áyək̓ʷ(ə)s

skunk VU pəpəc̓ín (cf. VU p̓céṅsət 'to get body odor')

otter VU sq̓éʔeƛ̓ ~ sq̓é(ʔ)eƛ̓

rat VU k̓ʷétən

mouse (or more likely, weasel) LD sɫc̓ém̓ (rare LD c̓)

mouse VU k̓ʷək̓ʷtəná·ɬ ("small rat offspring")

squirrel; chipmunk VU čəpsiyásən

rabbit LD həpít, VU lépət (< Engl.)

muskrat sq̓éɬq̓əɬ

pig VU kešú

sheep VU ləmətú

cow VU músməs

cat VU píšpiš, LD píš

(mountain) lion VU k̓ʷéyəčn

cougar LD ƛ̓éqtnč, VU ƛ̓éqtnəč

fox sməy̓áw ~ sməyáw (Swinomish dial. of Lushootseed said to share this form)

bat VU ɬəlp̓əléxən ("wrinkled wing")

bird (any kind) VU (s)c̓íc̓ec̓əm, LD,TB θíθəθəm

bald eagle, eagle k̓ʷéləŋsən

  osprey, fishhawk čé·nəxʷ k̓ʷéləŋsn

chicken hawk xəŋxénələ(?)

owl (any kind) čí·tŋəxʷ

small owl (any kind) spəlqʷíc̓a (rare LD c̓, in 'ghost', a related word, LD has
  c̓ ~ θ̓)

raven sk̓ʷtá?

crow sk̓ʷək̓ʷátə?

great blue heron snə́k̓ʷa?

duck má?aqʷ

mallard tə́nəqsn

brant xə́ɬxəɬč

goose ƛ̓ék̓ʷəxən

sawbill, merganser q̓ə́mət

black duck, surf scoter (way out in sea) čəwəčéxən

loon swák̓ʷən

cormorant, "shag" mésəč

seagull qʷəní

thick-billed murre (just seen in winter, far out) (VU) sx̣éyic̓

tufted duck; goldeneye; bufflehead xəx̣q̓əné?

greater scaup; c vasback; redhead duck x̣ə́ɬəlwəɬ

black diver (has white front) sxʷtís

kingfisher θəčə́lə?

woodpecker (both pileated and smaller) VU c̓íqt, LD θíqt

blue grouse ŋí?iƛ̓

willow grouse (ruffed grouse) (VU) sqʷə́c̓

bluejay čí·ye?

robin k̓ʷə́sqəq (this may be Saanich)

wren t̓ət̓ə́m̓

hummingbird (s)x̣ʷə́t̓čəli

pigeon həm̓ú

hair seal VU ʔésxʷ
sea lion VU ʔešés
whale VU qʷə́nəs
killer whale VU q̇əłáləmečn
porpoise VU k̇ʷánət, LD k̇ʷánṫ
jellyfish (large or small) VU šłáxʷ
  sea anemone šłáxʷ(s) tə sn̩énət ("jellyfish of the rock")
octopus VU sqé·ymək̇ʷ
large octopus VU píl·əwəs, also VU qəṁk̇ʷá·ł ("octopus offspring")
sea cucumber VU sík̇ʷt

shell LD čéwiẏ
crab VU ʔéčəx̣
red crab (some are big) kʷəkʷáƛ̇šn
barnacle VU ċəmáẏə
big sea urchin (purple or red with spines) VU x̣éxʷə (yellow part is eaten
  raw, if eat more than two in hot weather one gets dopey)
small green sea urchin VU sk̇ʷíciẏ (can be eaten like large ones)
butter clam VU sʔáx̣ʷaʔ
little necks (clams) VU (s)k̇ʷłé·ẏ ~ sk̇ʷłéʔeẏ
cockles VU sƛ̇(ə)láʔam
oyster VU ƛ̇áx̣ʷƛ̇əx̣ʷ
horse clam VU swém
mussel VU łéẇqəṁ
big chiton (grey) VU ʔák̇ʷəs (cooked and eaten, cook carefully or it gets
  rubbery)
small black chinese slippers (limpets) VU x̣é̇ləṁ (these have like teeth on
  the outside, can be eaten after cooking)

fish (any kind) VU sčé·nəxʷ (=TB)
spring salmon yáməč, (VU sċáqʷiʔ ~ sθáqʷiʔ prob. < Halkomelem)
coho salmon VU séẇən (corrected as Saanich), VU q̇éčəqs, LD q̇éčqs
sockeye salmon VU sə́qəẏ
dog salmon VU k̇ʷáɫəxʷ
humpback salmon VU hénəṅ
salmon after spawning (ready to die, male or female) VU x̣éɫəč
steelhead VU sx̣ə́ẇqəm, LD sx̣áẇqəm
trout (any kind) VU (s)k̇ʷsəč, LD k̇ʷsə́č
big bullhead (2 ft. long, cod-sized)(poss. 'grey cod') LD skʷənéxʷ
middle-sized bullhead LD sx̣ʷáyəwəč
small-sized bullhead (2 to 3 in.)(sculpin) VU sx̣ʷénəɫ, LD sx̣ʷə́ẏnəɫ
  (if from good clear water were eaten, not if by houses)
red cod (wide, about 2 ft. long) VU qʷtə́yəsn, LD qʷtáyəsən
ling cod, grey cod ʔéyət

rock cod LD ʔeyəsísəŋ

black cod (way out at sea) qʷémǝs

kelp cod (yellow, some black, some blue spotted, used as bait for large
  cod) p̓qʷíqǝn

cod eggs sx̣ə́yx̣ǝyx̣̓ (pick up and eat raw if fresh)

cod liver x̣̓q̓ʷə́ys

sole VU x̣̓ə́nǝq̓ʷa

flounder VU p̓ə́wǝy̓ (boiled to cook)

halibut sátx̣, sáʔtx̣ (boiled or fried to cook)

(fresh) herring sx̣̓á·ʔŋǝt

black bass, black rockfish LD syə́nyǝn̓xʷ ~ syə́nyǝn̓xʷ

red snapper LD tə́qʷtǝqʷ (come up to surface, die easy)

dogfish (never eaten, use skin for sandpaper) VU sk̓ʷéʔec̓ ~ k̓ʷéyič̓,
  LD k̓ʷéy(i)ǝ̓

shark (any kind)(not eaten) VU k̓ʷ(ə)c̓ǝnǝtčǝ, LD k̓ʷǝ̓ǝ̓ǝnǝx̣̌če

skate VU q̓éqǝw̓, LD sq̓éqǝw (just the arms, x̣̓élǝw̓, are eaten)

ratfish VU skʷámǝʔ, LD skʷáma (ratfish oil used for hair)

surf smelt qʷǝ́x̣̓ǝs (gotten from shore, eaten raw)

perch wéči? (lots by Anacortes, Washington, caught in chickenwire net
  trap)

fish like a grey cod sq̓ʷéʔ

grunt or singing fish (something like sǝmiyámǝ 'Semiahmoo')

snake VU sʔáx̣̓qaʔ ~ sʔáx̣̓qǝʔ, LD sʔáx̣̓qǝʔ (=TB)

rattlesnake VU k̓ʷétx̣ǝm̓nǝč

frog, bullfrog sx̣ǝʔénǝxʷ

  baby frog, tadpole sx̣ǝʔénǝxʷá·x̣̓

lizard, salamander VU pítšn̓

snail VU q̓ǝyáx̣̓ǝn̓

housefly VU qǝq̓ə́yǝx̣ǝnǝ

mosquito qʷéʔen

sand-fly pxʷíqsn

bee (any kind, bumble, etc.) VU smsmáy̓e

butterfly VU k̓ʷǝx̣̓k̓ʷǝx̣̓éx̣ǝn̓

spider VU qǝtčálǝ, LD qǝtqǝtčálǝʔ

daddy-long-legs LD sk̓ʷéy̓

ant VU čm̓cǝyí ("bites on big things")

worm (any kind) VU sc̓ǝ́k̓ʷ

caterpillar mǝmǝx̣éx̣̓

body louse; bedbug VU ŋǝ́sǝn̓, TB ŋǝ́sǝn

flea VU x̣̓átǝx̣ǝm̓

head louse; nits x̣ǝ́x̣ak̓ʷ

deer bug, deer tick, woodtick ŋǝ́sǝns tǝ smǝ́yis ("deer's louse" since caught
  from deer)

maggots VU šáy̓eʔ

pond frog that hollars at night VU wə́x̣əs

worm that gets inside berries VU č̓k̓ʷə́təŋ tə s?ə́łtənəŋ ("the berries are
  gotten inside of on purpose")

centipede VU łc̓íŋən sc̓ə́k̓ʷ, LD łθ́íŋən sθ́ə́k̓ʷ ("comb worm")

grasshopper x̌ʷəx̌ʷtəm̓iyáč (√'jumping', see VU x̌ʷítŋ 'jump')

powerful monster, creature with power to do harm (incl. any fierce water or
  land creatures like grizzly, snake, bear, killer whale, wolf, etc. and
  creatures like giants, wild small people, thunderbird, giant lizard-like
  creature, two-headed snake, sea monster in the Maiden of Deception Pass)
  sx̌́éləqəm

thunderbird sx̣ʷəx̣ʷá?as

two-headed snake č̓ə́sə sq̓ʷáŋi? s?á́łqa?

giant lizard-like creature that lives in a lake (if one sees it and tells
  one spits blood and dies) síneɫqəy̓

cannibal basket ogress LD θ̓əw̓x̣éləč, VU c̓əw̓x̣éləč

the Transformer x̣é?eɫs

(sasquatch, hairy giant in the Malahat range Cowichan Halkomelem VU c̓áməq̓ʷəs,
  LD θ̓áməq̓ʷəs)

(little strong people that live in wild, can knock over trees, if one sees
  them he gets sick unless he's purified himself (bathed, fasted, etc.)
  Cowichan Halkomelem VU,LD siy̓é·yɛ?, LD stí?tɛł)

Flora

tree sqəlélŋəxʷ

hemlock tree, "balsam" skʷéməyəqs (pulp wood is made out of this today)

big Douglas fir čséy̓

red cedar x̣péy̓

yellow cedar páš̌ələqʷ

alder sqʷán̓əɫč

maple (incl. big-leaf maple and vine maple) q̓ém̓əniɫč

yew ƛ̓əŋqíɫč (or ƛ̓əŋqéɫč)

willow sx̣ʷəlé?eɫč ~ sx̣ʷəlí?iɫč ("reef net plant")

  pussy willow sqʷəqʷem̓éy̓čis ("puppy in the hand")

arbutus qʷaqʷíɫč

prob. cottonwood or poplar (narrow at both ends, leaves shimmer, white wood
  used for paddles, never darkens) q̓ʷəy̓íləš̌əɫp ("dancing tree", prob.
  < Cowichan)

dogwood qʷítx̣əɫp (Cowichan, possibly also > Samish)

unidentified tree (kind of like cedar) VU pəpc̓əné̓y̓əɫp, LD pəθəné̓y̓əɫp
  ("body odor/skunk bark tree", poss. < Cowichan)

berry s?ə́ɫtənŋ (words for fruit add –íɫč to indicate the whole plant
  as in 'strawberry' and 'strawberry plant' for example)

wild berry of any kind TB,VU sčəlíqʷɫ

strawberry plant (wild or tame) LD t̓íləqʷíɫč

strawberry (fruit) t̓íləqʷ

raspberry; blackcap čilqʷámə?

soapberry, Indian ice cream sx̣ʷéysəm ~ sx̣ʷésəm ~ VU sx̣ʷésəŋ

gooseberry qém̓k̓ʷ

Indian currant xʷíxʷk̓ʷ

salmonberry ?əlílə?

salalberry t̓éqe?

cranberry qʷəm̓čáls

red elderberry VU c̓íwəq̓

swamp blueberry, Canada blueberry (low, 3 ft. high) ɫəw̓qím̓

tall swamp blueberry (prob. oval-leaf blueberry) mál̓sən̓

black huckleberry VU yíy̓i?x̣əm̓, LD yíy̓x̣əm

black to grey mountain huckleberry sčí?sən

red huckleberry VU (s)k̓ʷáqʷčis, LD sk̓ʷáqʷčis ("something clubbed on the
  hand")

thimbleberry t̓éqʷəm̓

short Oregon grape berry séni?

blackberry sk̓ʷəlélŋəxʷ

  wild blackberry t̓ál̓tələw̓ sk̓ʷəlélŋəxʷ

  domesticated blackberry š̌xʷənítəməɫ sk̓ʷəlélŋəxʷ ("white man-style blackberry")

black hawthorn berry méč̓ən̓

snowberry pəṗqeyá·s

crabapple LD qéʔexʷ, VU qé(ʔ)exʷ ~ qéyəxʷ (this latter said right after
   VU pronounced the Saanich word for 'crabapple' qéyəxʷ)

rose hip LD qə́ləq

wild rose qəlqíɫč (or qəlqéɫč)

June plum (first to blossom in spring, last to ripen, black fruit)
   VU c̓áxʷən̓ ~ c̓áxʷən, LD θ̓áxʷən

bitter cherry skʷə́θ̓əŋíɫč (bark used for basket decoration/imbrication)
   bitter cherry bark LD kʷə́θ̓ən̓

grass (domestic or wild) sáx̣ʷəl

sharp grass (prob. cut-grass Scirpus microcarpus)(used for baskets?)
   pšéy̓

white straw grass from swamp (used for baskets, mats, etc.) ƛ̓ə́ƛ̓

cattail reed VU sc̓éqən, LD sθ̓éqən̓ (q⁻ʔq for both)

bulrush reed sqʷéləɫ

underwater grass (plant with red leaves that grows on rocks in sea but
   sticks up out of water, maybe a kind of seaweed) k̓ʷéqəq

skunk cabbage VU (s)c̓ák̓ʷiy̓, LD θ̓ák̓ʷiy̓

cow parsnip yáləʔ

turnip VU šxʷʔiléwəʔ, LD šxʷʔiléwaʔ (< Chinook Jargon)

carrots (wild or domestic) šéwəq
   "wild carrot", spring-gold (from photo in Turner 1975) ƛ̓ə́ɫt̓ələw̓ šéwəq

potato (wild or domestic) sqéws

camas (gathered by some on Flattop Is. called qé·y̓mək̓ʷəŋ, west of Orcas Is.)
   VU qʷƚál, VU spánxʷ, LD qʷƚáʔal

onions ʔən̓yəns (< English)
   wild onions ƛ̓ə́ɫt̓ələw̓ ʔən̓yəns
   poss. wild onion (LD heard her mother say this word) q̓ʷə́xʷiʔəč

nettles VU c̓ə́xc̓əx, LD θ̓ə́xθ̓əx

red weed of some kind (for ex. grows along shore of Orcas Is. between
   Rosario and Orcas ferry landing) VU q̓ʷáq̓ʷəqʷ

devil's club q̓ʷáʔpəɫp (prob. < Cowichan)

red osier dogwood (bark is eye medicine) VU sx̣ʷəlé·ɫč, LD sx̣ʷəlíʔiɫč
   (but this form is the same as given above for 'willow'; the root is
   sx̣ʷálə 'reef net' suggesting that the plant was used for making reef nets,
   and it's unlikely red osier dogwood bark could be so used)

Indian consumption plant q̓əx̣mín

ironwood, oceanspray (used for salmon barbecue sticks) VU q̓éc̓əɫč ~
   q̓ə́y̓c̓əɫč, LD q̓éy̓c̓ɫč (or prob. q̓éy̓əɫč)

Indian tea plant, Labrador tea tihíɫč (root < English 'tea')

plantain sx̣əʔénəxʷiɫč ("frog plant")

bracken fern (used to eat roots) səqé·n (also 'lady fern; spiny wood fern')

licorice fern (add to any medicine to kill the taste of other ingredients)

ɬəsíp
sword fern; male fern (used for new dancers) sx̌éləm
giant horsetail fern sx̌ém̓x̌əm̓
green moss on rock or tree q̓áči?
green sprouts in spring, new soft leaf tips on end of branches (grows on
    all trees except alder and maple) sməx̌t̓éləs (cognate in Upriver
    Halkomelem means 'grey/green hanging tree moss)
white hanging lichen that grows on alder VU sqṗíqʷəs, LD sqṗíqʷs
mushroom (never heard of it being eaten) LD k̓ʷəm̓stəlí?qʷ
get mouldy VU pápəqʷ

kelp VU q̓ʷá·ŋ
    kelp ribbons VU siyétənəɬ q̓ʷáŋ
green seaweed that grows on the bottom like on sandbars, grows in thin
    strips, where crabs are often found) VU čéləm
green seaweed VU ɬə́q̓əs
red seaweed VU ɬəɬq̓ə́t ɬə́q̓əs
underwater grass (listed under grasses above) may belong here

underbrush sk̓ʷáyima?
tree trunk and roots, stump, snag VU x̌eyə́m̓nəč, LD x̌əyə́m̓nəč
roots VU q̓ʷəč̓əŋ, LD q̓ʷəθ̓əŋ
cedar roots VU x̌peẏíɬč q̓ʷəč̓əŋ
cedar bough sč̓é?sən̓
cedar bark (esp. inner bark) sléwəẏ ~ sléwiẏ
bitter cherry bark LD k̓ʷəθ̓əŋ̓
bark of fir or "balsam" (hemlock), any bark č̓éləẏ ~ č̓éleẏ (=TB)
fine sharp stuff (from dead fir bark) VU sc̓ísəɬ, LD sθ̓ísəɬ
fir cone, pine cone ṗéyšəč
limb of a tree, knot in a tree or wood, knothole VU sc̓éyst ~ sc̓éyst
lump (on a tree, person, ground, etc.) VU spápəkʷ, LD spápkʷ
leaf VU sc̓ác̓əɬa?, LD sθ̓áθ̓(ə)ɬə?, TB sθ̓áθ̓ɬe
flower sk̓ʷíqəŋ, TB sk̓ʷéqəŋ
rotten tree, rotten wood pqʷə́ẏ
dead tree still in the ground st̓ét̓čiẏ
pitch VU smánič, LD smánəč
    pitchwood sma?án̓č

The Body
the whole body VU s(ə)ɬtélŋəxʷ, LD sɬtéləŋəxʷ
head sq̓ʷáŋi? (=TB)
top of the head, crown VU q̓təlí?qʷ, LD šq̓ətəlí?qʷ (VU says this may
    be a slang term, see also 'roof')
skull VU c̓əmí?qʷ, LD sθ̓əmí?qʷ
back of the head, back of the neck téčsŋ (=TB)

forehead sq̓ʷə́ŋəs

eyebrow sáŋən

eyelash ɬə́ptən

eye qélə̓ŋ, TB qéləŋ

nose ŋə́qsən (=TB)

bridge of nose VU šc̓əmə́ləqsən, LD š̓ə̓əmə́ləqsən

tip of nose poss. sx̣əpqʷéləqsən

nostrils LD š̓ɬlqʷélqsn (this may be Cowichan)

face sʔásəs

half of the face šɬq̓ás

ear q̓ʷélə̓ŋ (=TB)

mouth sásən (=TB but TB ~ θáθən)

upper lip słásən

lower lip and jaw ƛ̓čásən

jawbone LD sə̓əmásən

tongue VU tíx̣ʷsəɬ, LD tíx̣ʷsɬ

tooth čə́nəs

uvula mə́l̓qʷ

throat x̣ʷáŋən

inside throat, gullet šqənx̣ʷélə

shoulder LD qʷəqʷíʔqŋ̓

arm ƛ̓éləw̓

hand séləs (=TB)

wristbone sqʷəm̓x̣ʷés·

elbow VU sc̓əməléx̣ə̓ŋ, LD sə̓əməléx̣ə̓ŋ

armpit šx̣ʷƛ̓əqʷəléx̣ən

finger ?

index finger šx̣ʷʔəkʷsíl̓s ("pointing thing, pointer")

your palm sʔásəs· tə̓ŋ séləs ("face of your hand")

fingernail VU c̓šálsəs, LD c̓šáls·

knuckle VU c̓əmésəs, LD θ̓əmés(ə)s ~ sə̓əmés·

collarbone x̣ƛ̓ínəsən

chest VU c̓ə́ŋəɬ, LD θ̓ə́ŋəɬ

chest bone spətínəs, VU c̓əmínəs, LD š̓ə̓əmínəs

breast (woman or man), nipple, milk sqəmá?

side of the body (human or not) šx̣ʷʔíləx̣ən

shoulderblade qʷəqʷíʔqən

right arm and hand sʔiyáləmíw̓s

left arm and hand VU c̓əkʷəʔíw̓s, LD sə̓əkʷəʔíw̓s

ribs VU lə́kʷəx̣, LD lə́kʷx̣

belly k̓ʷélə (vs. Saanich VU ƛ́és (=TB))

belly-button, navel mə́x̣ʷəye?

back VU stéskʷəɬ (=TB), LD stéskʷɬ

backbone VU sc̓əmáɬən, LD sə̓əmáɬən

buttocks and upper leg słáləč (=TB 'leg')

penis; urinate šəšíwaʔ
testicles ŋésən
vagina LD séwəɬ
anus šqəʔéŋəṅ
leg and foot sx̣énəʔ, TB sx̣éneʔ 'foot'
knee sqék̇ʷəŋ
calf and ankle qʷéməx̣ʷsṅ ("lump on leg/foot")
leg bone sθámsən
your sole šx̣ásəs təṅ sx̣énəʔ
toe ?
toenail (only Saanich known čsálsən)
heel on bottom VU sċátəẇič, LD sθátəẇič

hair on head síʔetn, TB siyétən
grey hair sx̣áləməs
curly hair VU sq̇əlpíʔqʷ, (s)q̇əlq̇élpəs
bald headed šq̇ʷəwəlíqʷ
hair in the nose šqʷənéləqsən
beard qʷíṅsən
hair on the body (under arms, on chest, legs, on arms) VU qʷínəkʷəs,
  LD qʷín(ə)kʷs
pubic hair qʷínəq
hair on rump VU šqʷənéwəč

brains VU sméċqn ~ šméċqəṅ, LD sméθqn ~ šméθqəṅ
heart VU ċéləʔ, LD,TB θéləʔ
all the insides šnəẇíkʷən
guts q̇əq̇əý
stomach (inside organ) VU ċsáʔ, LD θsáʔ
liver ƛ̇éqəʔ, TB ƛ̇éqeʔ
lungs LD spélxʷəṅ ~ spéləxʷəṅ
bladder poss. šxʷiyélə
blood séščən (=TB but TB ~ θéščən)
bone VU sċám, LD sθám, TB sθám
marrow VU sċəċéšsṅ, LD θəθéšsən
flesh sɬíqʷ, smáyis
muscle ƛ̇íʔiŋən
skin, hide k̇ʷéləẇ (=TB)
  skin on face is hanging loose VU sɬəlɬélpəs
joints (bends) of the bone VU sq̇ʷəʔáləs tə sċám
fat, grease VU nás
snot šmétəqsən
dung LD sq̇ʷəq̇ʷəθ̇
a tear šqáʔas
a cut VU q̇émtən

a cold VU sċáłŋ

a cough VU stáq̓ʷŋ

breath słék̓ʷŋ (=TB)

  to breathe TB łék̓ʷən

thoughts, feelings VU šqʷéləkʷən

smell it háqʷnəxʷ, TB háqʷət

taste it ƛ̓éʔet

hear TB ləléʔŋ

see it, see someone VU léŋnəxʷ, LD léŋənəxʷ

feel it, feel someone VU ƛ̓épət, LD ƛ̓épt

to sweat VU čáq̓ʷŋ

  sweating VU čáʔq̓ʷṇ

to spit čx̣ʷáłs, TB čx̣ʷéłθe

  spitting čx̣ʷáʔłs

   to spit on something čx̣ʷət

swallow it VU ŋq̓ət, LD ŋəq̓ət

to sneeze VU hésŋ

snoring łəƛ̓áq̓ʷən

to eat ʔíłən (=TB)

to bite TB θə́ŋət

to run VU kʷániŋət

to crawl čtə́ŋ

to walk štə́ŋ

to step on something ʔíŋət

to stand TB síłəŋ

  standing səsíłəṇ

to sleep VU,TB ʔítət, LD ʔítt

to wake up VU xʷəčəsət, LD xʷəčəst

come to one's senses (as child or adult), be sober; hatch p̓əł

to talk, speak, say VU,TB q̓ʷél

to laugh nə́čəŋ

to be pregnant sk̓ʷéy̓k̓ʷiy̓

to swell up (belly, tide, etc.) VU p̓áŋ

to get bruised ƛ̓áqaʔ

  (get) a black eye VU šƛ̓əqaʔáləs

to live, be alive helí (=TB) ~ həlí

to die TB q̓ʷáy

to be sick VU ʔəsx̣éłəł

it is hurting VU séčən(s) (n maybe sic for ŋ)

to get hurt VU méʔkʷəł, LD méʔkʷł

to get scalded VU k̓ʷəsíkʷəs

to get fits VU sq̓éq̓əƛ̓

to be crazy VU sxʷéʔxʷəkʷ

coughing VU táq̓ʷṇ

shivering VU łə́txtəṇ

shaking   VU čə́nəŋ
to vomit   čé?et (=TB)
to urinate; penis   šəšíwa?
to defecate   VU q̓ʷə́c̓ ~ q̓ʷəq̓ʷə́c̓ ~ pé
to weep, cry   x̣ʷáŋ (=TB)
to fly   kʷə́ləŋ (=TB)

long feather   VU sƛ̓qé?en ~ šƛ̓qé·n̓
fine down feather (like duck's for pillow)   VU sƛ̓pél̓qən̓, ƛ̓pél̓qən
feather   TB st̓áq̓ʷ
wing (bird, bat, skate), arm   t̓éləw̓
egg   ?ég, ?éks (< English)
shell   LD čéwiy
horn, antler   VU c̓ístn
soft edible bone in fish head   sx̣ə́pəkʷ
nose of human/animal/fish   ŋə́qsən
eye (of any creature)   qə́ləŋ̓
jaw (of any creature)   ƛ̓čásən
gills   VU šé?iy, LD šé?iy̓
gill bone   x̣ƛ̓ínəsən   (see 'collarbone' above)
fin below gills   q̓étŋən
fin on top of back, (also) killer whale's top fin   sq̓éw̓əčən̓
   killer whale's/blackfish's top fin   sq̓éw̓čən̓s tə qəlƛ̓áləməčən
backbone (of human, fish, animal, etc.)   VU sc̓əmáɬən, LD sə̇əmáɬən
head (of any creature)   sq̓ʷáŋi?
fish slime   stíšəm
fish liver   ƛ̓q̓ʷə́y̓
liver (of deer, animal, human. bird)   VU t̓éqa?, LD t̓éqə?
fish eggs   qə́ləx̣ (=TB 'salmon eggs')
milt   ƛ̓k̓ʷí?
blood all together along belly where you open a fish   št̓qə?íqən̓
air bladder?, long tube like a balloon in fish   špə́xʷ
fish heart   mə́l̓qʷ
oil (of fish or anything)   snás
eulachon oil   ƛ̓ína?   (loan-word)
to render oil (boil till oil comes out)   snəséləqən
fish cheek ("ear of the fish")   q̓ʷə́ləŋ̓s tə sčé·nəxʷ
fish skin   k̓ʷə́ləw̓s tə sčé·nəxʷ
barbecued fish head   q̓ʷəlíqʷ
whole smoked herring   sk̓ʷsím
open smoked herring   sk̓ʷə́l̓č
herring eggs (eaten raw)   čə́məš
stink eggs (fish eggs put in flour sack now and hung over the smoke in a
   smokehouse; it can be cut like cheese when ready)   spá?
cod eggs (eaten raw if fresh)   sx̣ə́yx̣əyƛ̓

fish eggs hung in an air bladder šəpəlíwəʔ
fish air bladder taken out (can be filled with eggs from same fish and
   doesn't make stink eggs, hung up not buried) VU čsáʔ, LD q̇sáʔ
fish eggs in a barrel sƛ̇əmk̇ʷ
whole smoked fish sx̣éč sčéʔenəxʷ

Human Relations
person VU ʔəłtélŋəxʷ, LD ʔəłtélənəxʷ, TB ʔełtélŋəxʷ, (prob. √ʔełtí 'here')
woman, female słéniʔ
man, male VU swéy̓əqaʔ, LD swéy̓qaʔ, TB swéyəqə
old person, elder (also used for parent) sʔéləxʷ
child VU sƛ̇íƛ̇əƛ̇qəł (=TB) ~ sƛ̇íƛ̇qəł, LD sƛ̇íƛ̇əƛ̇qł
   children VU stéwixʷəł, LD sté·xʷəł
baby VU qəqéq, LD qéq
young boy VU swiw̓ləsá·ł, LD swiw̓ləs(h)áł
young girl VU słeničá·ł, LD słenčá·ł
teenaged boy swíw̓ələs
teenaged girl q̇éy̓ŋiʔ
   young girl (11 or 12, pre-teen) VU q̇əŋičá·ł ~ q̇əŋičá·ł

relative (any sex or age) šxʷáq̇waʔ (TB šxʷʔáq̇wəʔ 'brother')
to be related together VU ʔəq̇ʷéy̓təł, LD ʔəq̇ʷíy̓təł
husband swéy̓qəʔ ("man")
spouse stál·əs, TB stáləs 'husband'
to marry, get a spouse VU čtáləs
husband/wife (slang), "other half" VU snác̓əʔ ~ snáθ̇əʔ
father mén (=TB)
mother tén (=TB)
mommy, Ma, (can also be used for small children) téʔ
daddy, Dad méʔ
lots of parents (sg. uncertain) səléʔsət, LD also séləʔst
offspring, child of someone ŋénəʔ
   my son nə ŋénəʔ
   my daughter LD snə ŋénəʔ
older sibling, cousin through ancestor's older sibling šéyeł
   older siblings šəšé·yəł
younger sibling, cousin through ancestor's younger sibling VU səy̓íčn̓,
   LD səy̓ečn̓
   younger siblings səlé·ʔčn
oldest child in family láƛ̇
youngest child in family VU həhé·ʔič, LD héʔič
nephew, niece stíkʷən
   my nephew nə stíkʷən
   my niece sə nə stíkʷən
grandparent VU sílaʔ, LD síl·aʔ

grandparents səlsílaʔ
grandchild ʔínəs
grandparent-in-law šxʷsíləʔ
great grandparent, great grandchild čáməqʷ
great great grandparent, (great great grandchild) VU čə́payəqʷ, LD ʔə́kʷiyəqʷ
great great great grandparent, (great great great grandchild) VU ʔə́kʷiyəqʷ,
    LD θə́payəqʷ
ancestors, elders, old people sʔəɫéləxʷ
mother's brother's wife VU sŋétxʷəns, LD sŋétxʷns (prob. has -s 'his/her')
    vs. husband's brother, wife's sister sŋétxʷən
uncle's wife, aunt's husband šxʷsécs
parent-in-law, sibling-in-law slé·ɫ ~ sléʔeɫ
    all one's in-laws VU sləɫléʔeɫ, LD səlsəléʔeɫ
parent's sibling sécs
deceased parent's sibling VU qsəčéləɫ, LD qsəčé·ɫ
wife's sister's husband snəčélnəq ~ snčélnəq
husband's brother's wife LD šxʷʔéləs
    vs. wife's cousin's wife VU šxʷʔéləš
widow, widower siyéʔtən (cf. síʔetən 'hair on head' due to custom of
    burning one's hair to mourn a lost spouse)
orphan kʷénəŋ
adopted child sk̓ʷə́ŋeʔɫ̓ŋ
half-sibling VU snəčéwəɫ, LD snčéwəɫ
spouse of deceased sibling čé·ẏə
    to marry spouse of deceased sibling čéẏeŋ
step-parent LD s·ʔák̓ʷəɫ, VU šxʷs·ʔák̓ʷəɫ corrected to sʔák̓ʷəɫ
deceased child VU ʔək̓ʷə́čəɫ, my deceased child LD ʔn sʔək̓ʷə́čɫ
your child's spouse ʔn̓ sčiwté·ɫ
child of deceased sibling VU skʷə́nəŋəčəɫ, LD skʷə́nŋəčɫ
two wives, co-wives, husband of ex-wife, wife of ex-husband sáyeʔ
    two wives fighting LD səʔáẏsiyeʔ
to have a child čŋénəʔ
have an illegitimate child ʔəw̓ čŋénəʔ nəsʔal

raise someone k̓ʷə́ŋət
loving each other ƛ̓íƛ̓ətəl
looking after one another ləŋátəl
jealous pəsténəq
high class person, leader, boss siẏém̓
poor person stə́səs
slave sk̓ʷə́yis
ashamed to take a slave sɫíɫiẏ̓
my friend nə sčéʔčeʔ
    my dear friends siyém̓ nə sčéləčeʔ
enemy šəmén

to get raided tə́q ("closed")

  to raid (by canoe) tqénəq

to make war x̣éləx̣

warrior VU stáməš

name VU,TB sné

ancestral name nəhé·mət

nick-name kʷšémən̓

insult someone's body, call someone a dirty name VU psə́kʷt (kʷ ~ qʷ)

village ʔéɬənənəkʷ

white man, non-Indian VU xʷənítəm ~ xʷənítəm̓

watchman wéčmən (< English)

The Spirit·

soul səlí

guardian spirit, a spirit power VU sʔə́ylə, LD sʔəylə, skʷiṅáŋət

spirit song (and its dance) syə́wən

an Indian dance, a spirit dance smíɬə

  to spirit dance míɬə

new spirit dancer, "baby" x̌əẃsálkʷɬ ("new spirit power")

bear spirit power speʔesálkʷɬ

a spirit dancer (new or old), Indian dancer sčə́ɬx̌ʷəṅ

a long-time Indian dancer ƛ̓ə́lŋəč čyíwəṅ

paint one's face VU ɬx̌ásŋ

  paint one's face with charcoal VU ɬx̌ásŋ kʷ číct

Indian doctor, medicine man, shaman šnéʔem, VU šx̌ʷnéʔem

to cure someone (of Indian doctors or Indian Shakers) VU ɬékʷət, LD ɬékʷt

power to kill or do harm q̓ʷčíŋəɬ

shoot power into someone (done by an Indian doctor) LD x̣t̓ələʔ

train for something (canoe racing/["canoe pulling"], Indian doctoring, sport,
    spirit dancing, etc.) VU t̓éy̓əsət ~ t̓əy̓əsət

  training for something VU t̓éy̓t̓əsət, LD t̓át̓əst

training for Indian doctoring/spirit dancing/or one's own health LD k̓ʷəčást

have a funeral for someone VU mék̓ʷəɬtxʷ

person who does ritual burnings (for the dead and their friends + relations)
  LD čqʷíls

brushing a longhouse/a person/a home (done by a ritualist after a death)
  šičqʷí·leʔ

person who reads minds or predicts the future syə́ẉə

person who talks to spirits/ghosts VU pəɬqʷicəʔálkʷɬ, LD spəlqʷíθəʔalkʷɬ

power boards, sgʷədíləč boards skʷəníleč

medicine VU st̓élŋəxʷ, LD st̓élənəxʷ

use medicine on someone t̓əlŋíxʷt

taboo, forbidden VU sx̣éʔx̣a, LD sx̣éʔx̣a(ʔ)

Entertainment

to dance (Indian or non-Indian style) q̓ʷəyíləš

  dancing VU q̓ʷəy̓íləš, LD q̓ʷəy̓íləš

to play VU həṁnéʔ, TB həmənéʔ

the bone game, slahal game ləhéɬ

  playing slahal (gambling) ləhéʔeɬ

  slahal bones (all four) VU sləhéɬ

  to guess the outside bones (in slahal) VU píq̓ət

  to guess the inside bones (in slahal); to dive in VU néqən

  my bet VU nə sákʷəla?

to guess something VU t̓émət

to sing TB t̓íləm

  singing VU t̓ət̓íləṁ, LD t̓íləṁ

a song (any kind, spiritual or secular) stíləm

lullaby LD hanáy̓ɫ

a story/legend from way back; rock with a spirit in it VU sx̣ʷiy̓im̓,
  LD sx̣ʷiy̓im̓ (second i ~ ə)

  telling a story/legend VU x̣ʷəx̣ʷəy̓im̓, LD x̣ʷəx̣ʷəy̓im̓ (i ~ ə)

a true story LD ʔəw̓ səʔít sqʷə́lqʷəl

a made-up story VU x̣ʷqéyəxqən̓ sqʷə́lqʷəl

  telling a made-up story LD qeyəxqə́y̓nən̓ ʔal

canoe-racing VU tétəy̓, LD tétiy̓

horse-race (or having a horse-race) VU c̓əc̓íli̓ʔtəl, LD θəθíli̓ʔtəl

have a tug-of-war x̣ʷəx̣ʷək̓ʷá·t (√'drag')

Man-made Things

 Buildings

house ʔéləŋ

dance-hall VU q̓ʷəyíləšewtxʷ, LD q̓ʷəyíləšewxʷ

spirit-dance house VU miɫəhéw̓txʷ ~ miɫəʔéw̓txʷ, LD miɫəhéw̓xʷ

roof outside; (slang for) top of the head šq̓təlíqʷ

wall (outside or inside) t̓áŋən

big beam in longhouse, ceiling beam šx̣ək̓ʷíɫən

housepost (inside or out) qéqən

board lapláš (< Chinook Jargon)

window VU šk̓ʷənásəŋ̓, LD šk̓ʷənásəm

fireplace čqʷə́w̓selə

doorway, door, road, path, highway sáɫ (=TB)

dirt floor (esp. of longhouse); bed šx̣ʷʔám̓ət

floor (wood, linoleum) VU ɫəx̣ənéptn, LD ɫəx̣énəptn

smoke vent, smoke hole šp̓áƛəŋs tə ʔéləŋ

protection from rain/wind/sun VU q̓ə́ləč(ə)sət, LD q̓ə́ləčst

cat-tail/bulrush wall mat sáleč

mat for floor/clothing/canoe/sleeping VU sɫéwən, LD šɫéwən

door-mat, something to wipe feet on VU šx̣ʷʔíčəsənəŋ, LD ? (š)x̣ʷʔíčəsənəŋ

pipe stove, pipe šp̓əƛən̓élə

pipe (for stove or tobacco) VU péʔek̓ʷ

back of house (inside or out, just the house itself) VU čələqʷéw̓txʷ ~
  čələqʷéw̓txʷ, LD čələqʷéw̓xʷ

front of house including land to the water VU c̓ítəs ~ θítəs, LD θítəs

bottom of house VU ƛ̓céw̓txʷ, LD ƛ̓céw̓xʷ

go around in a circle outside a house VU šələčéwtxʷ, LD šələčéwxʷ

  go around in a circle, to circle šáləč

go toward a fire VU híw̓əl tə sčəqʷə́w̓sə, LD híw̓əl tə sčəqʷəw̓(sə)

  go/come toward híw̓əl

go away from the fire VU qʷsécŋ tə sčəqʷə́w̓s, LD qʷsécŋ ʔə tə sčəqʷəw̓

cross the floor (inside longhouse), cross a river šáqʷəl

pit house, potato house, potato pit VU sčən̓éwtxʷ, LD sčń̓éwxʷ

a pole   sx̌t̓ək̓ʷəŋ
  carving a pole   VU x̌ə́t̓(ə)k̓ʷŋ, LD x̌ə́t̓k̓ʷŋ
fence   q̓əléx̌ən
smoking shed, fish smokehouse   VU pək̓ʷiŋəɬéwtx̌ʷ ~ q̓elə?éwtx̌ʷ,
  LD pək̓ʷiŋəɬéwx̌ʷ ~ q̓eléwx̌ʷ
longhouse   VU x̌ʷəx̌ʷilŋəx̌ʷéwtx̌ʷ   ("Indian house")
log house   VU čeləmənéwtx̌ʷ, LD čéɬəmənéwx̌ʷ
gravehouse, graveyard, grave   šməɬk̓ʷélə
funeral home   VU mek̓ʷə?éwtx̌ʷ
school   VU sk̓ʷúl (< English)
tent   VU siléwtx̌ʷ ~ siléwtx̌ʷ (free var.), LD siléwx̌ʷ

  Inventory
stuff, belongings   VU ?éwk̓ʷ
suitcase, trunk   šx̌ʷ?əwk̓ʷélə
box   ƛ̓áyəqs
lid, cover   VU q̓pəléyčən, LD q̓pəlíčən
key   VU ləkəlí   (< Chinook Jargon)
barrel   t̓əmə́w̓lič [t̓əmó?lɪč]
sack   lisék (< Chinook Jargon)
bed   šx̌ʷ?áṁət (VU also Saanich šx̌ʷ?ítət)
feather bed; down feathers   sk̓pélqŋ
blanket (any kind)   səmí?
goat wool blanket   swə́wq̓ʷəɬ [swóq̓ʷəɬ]
material, cloth   síl (< Chinook Jargon)
velvet   VU təmsə́ləqən
table   VU lətém   (< Chinook Jargon)
chair   sθəwéčn
cushion   VU sƛ̓íƛ̓pelqəṅ (i ~ ə), LD sk̓pélqən
big poker for logs in longhouse fire   šléləqsn
cooking pot   šq̓ʷéls
wooden/bone spoon, soapberry spoon   VU sx̌éləw̓, LD x̌éɬəw̓
horn spoon   VU ċístn x̌éɬəw̓
fork   LD mət̓əsítən
knife (any kind, carving wood or meat)   šípən
knife; cross-cut saw   VU ɬíčən
barbecue stick   pí?k̓ʷən
fish spreader   t̓é?ečən
dishes, plates   VU šx̌ʷ?íɬəṅ
plate; dishpan   lá?sn
  little plate, saucer   lála?sṅ
feast dish   q̓ʷsá·ləs
wash dishes, wash a canoe   VU ċək̓ʷk̓ʷí·la?, LD θək̓ʷk̓ʷí·la?
comb   VU ɬčíŋən, LD ɬθíŋən
  tooth of a comb   LD čə́nəs tə ɬθíŋən

a brush šx̌ʷʔəwpə́lqəṅ

fine-toothed comb špəxʷíʔqʷəŋ

broom VU šx̌ʷʔəx̌ʷísət, LD šx̌ʷʔəx̌ʷíst

ladder VU šk̓ʷí(y)šətn ~ (š)k̓ʷə́y̓šətəṅ, LD šk̓ʷí(y)štn

bucket sqʷáʔtn

tub t̓əmúʔləč

  washtub VU t̓əmúʔləč čk̓ʷə́l̓kʷətṅ, LD t̓əmúʔləč θ̓k̓ʷə́l̓kʷətṅ

bottle šləmélə

basketry cradle VU p̓áčəs, LD p̓áθ̓s

mirror; window LD šk̓ʷənásəṁ

phonograph, record player qʷlá·ysətəṅ

pipe šp̓əl̓əŋélə

purse, wallet štələhélə

eyeglasses štələháləs

cane, dancer's staff q̓ə́kʷə

deer hoofs and hoof rattle kʷəčmín

drum; drumstick VU q̓áwət

  drumming q̓aw̓étṅ

 Clothing

clothes; dress łqét (=TB)

  put on clothes VU ʔíčəŋ, LD ʔíθ̓ən

shirt VU šƛ̓píw̓əṅ, LD šƛ̓píw̓əṅ

pants səqíws

coat kəpú (< Chinook Jargon)

skirt LD ƛ̓íƛəptən

underskirt ƛčíkʷən

underwear VU ƛ̓číkʷən, LD šƛ̓číkʷən

shoe VU qʷłíʔšən, LD qʷłíʔšn

  put one one's shoes LD qʷłiʔšə́nəŋ

hat ?

  put on one's hat LD yása ʔqʷŋ

  take off one's hat LD łiŋáw̓əqʷŋ

moccasin LD sƛ̓ə́qšn

woolen knit knee-high stocking for spirit dancers ləmətéys

  put on your wool stockings VU t̓éyim̓t tṅ ləmətéys

stocking LD stékən (< English or Chinook Jargon)

put it on (of clothes of any kind, shoes, pants, hat, etc., poss. of

  non-clothing items too) t̓éyim̓t

mittens θ̓qʷáləče?

belt ƛ̓θ̓əyčən

bracelet sθ̓áməčən

necklace sqʷínqʷən

anything one has on one's neck (cloth, neckerchief, necklace, etc.)

  sx̌ʷíx̌ʷq̓ʷlnəł

earring sk̓ə́wəṅ ~ LD sk̓ə́wən
finger ring VU šx̌ʷyə́ləmčis, LD šyə́ləmčis (both ə=[í] poss. /í/)
(inner) cedar bark headdress for any dancer VU slə́wey̓ ƛq̓é?təs,
   LD slə́wey̓ ƛq̓é?ts
winter spirit dancer's whole costume sáčəkʷəs
cedar-bark skirt slə́wəy̓ ƛíƛəptṅ
shawl ləšál (< Chinook Jargon)

 Tools of Hunting, Fishing, Gathering, War, Weaving
bow yə́čət [yíčət]
arrow VU c̓əmé·ṅ, LD θ̓əmé·ṅ
war spear šx̌ʷəmá?tən
fish spear (either three-prong or two prong)(to spear fish or send down
   cod lure) VU c̓x̌áŋən, LD θ̓x̌áŋən
one-pointed shorter spear (with rope to pull it out with, used on seal
   or on land) té?eƛ
gun VU sk̓ʷəlíš [sk̓ʷəl?íš]
cod lure skʷíq̓əp (once ~ sqʷíqəp, once ~ sq̓ʷíqəp)
fish club slém̓əs
war club k̓ʷqʷástn ("club face device, something made to club face")
net (for fish or animals)(incl. gill net, purse seiner, drag net, etc.)
    swə́ltən [swíltən]
   when fish get caught in a gill net VU šwíwəq̓
purse seiner ?á?x̌ʷey̓ən
reef net sx̌ʷálə?
trap, deadfall trap x̌ə́šən
small scoop fish net (for fish, crabs, anything in the sea)(hoop made out
   of oceanspray wood and woven cedar bark, now of white man's net) ?ək̓ʷín
to fish for herring (use a herring rake) ƛə́ċəm̓
   fishing for herring ƛé?ċəm̓
   (cf. 'scattering it (of a fire) [raking it]' VU ƛéċət, LD ƛéċt)
bait (for animal or fish trap) ŋéḷŋəḷ
anchor ƛqəné?tən
   anchored (of boat or net) sƛəqəné?
   anchored net sƛəqəné? swə́ltn
big round fish trap (used in ocean) tqíp
fish weir šx̌éƛ
harpoon šmə́q̓tn
fish hook k̓ʷúyəkʷ
gaff hook ƛík̓ʷən
halibut hook səmáṅə(?)
fishing rod; fishing boat pé?e(y)čən
sinker line (used only for ling cod, dropped on bottom then pulled up while
   canoe is travelling); lead weight; bullet šét
a float p̓íp̓kʷtən

to open a fish   VU k̓ʷícət, LD k̓ʷíθt
knife   šípən
needle   VU čéyc̓ŋ, LD čéyθ̓ŋ
awl   VU šsəłqʷíŋəł, LD səłqʷíŋəł
  make a hole in it   słə́qʷt
  a hole   sə́łqʷ
a file (prob. a stone in pre-contact times)   čqə́ṅ
a hammer   hémən
maul, sledge hammer   VU mál
whetstone   (VU Saanich š̓t̓áqəs)
  he's sharpening it   t̓əqá?stəs
white man's wedge   wéǰ   (< English)
digging stick   sqéləx̣
plow   VU ƛ̓šə́nəp
to hunt   TB ?əmní?iŋ
to kill   TB q̓ʷáčət
pit-lamping (hunting by torchlight for animals or in canoe by torchlight
  for crabs, etc.)   héɫx̣əẇe
to get fish/berries/etc.   VU čqə́če?
  my catch   VU nə sqə́če?
cooking in a steam pit (usu. in sand on beach)(for clams, mussels, crabs,
  camas, not heard of for fish)   čə́nəst, also VU čə́nəst 'cook with steam'
  a steam-pit   VU c̓x̣ʷés, poss. LD θ̇x̣ʷés

wool; work   šč̓éy
old-fashioned wool-spinner   sə́lsəltn
modern wool-spinner   šqé·ləč̓ [šqé·lɪč̓]
a wool-carder   VU (s)təšéɫqəṅ, LD stəšéɫqəṅ
loom   (EU Cowichan   šx̣ʷ?əq̇əwélθ̇e)
to sew   TB čéθ̇ət
rope   VU x̣ʷéyləṁ, LD x̣ʷéyləṁ
  string, twine   x̣ʷəx̣ʷéyləṁ
tumpline, packstrap   LD səṅá?tn
loose-weave basket   məháẏ
  I'm making a basket   LD ?ən čéyə θə məháẏ
tight-weave cedar-root basket (for berries, etc.), water-tight basket   spč̓á?
cedar-slat basket   LD k̓ʷək̓ʷi?x̣ʷáləs
berry basket   LD šθ̇ə́məntəṅ
big storage basket   šx̣ʷ?əwk̓ʷélə məháẏ

 Transportation
canoe (esp. a small one), car   snə́x̣ʷəł
biggest canoe   VU ?átx̣əs, LD ?átx̣s
big canoe (smaller than ?átx̣əs)   q̇x̣ʷə́ẇł   (prob. < Cowichan)
crosspiece in canoe   VU x̣éləwəł

bow of canoe híʔiw
stern of canoe skʷéʔet
mast, sail pole, pole and the sail on it špaxʷəŋélə
sail; rag páxʷən
rudder of boat šq̓ayénč
canoe paddle VU sq̓éməl̓, LD sq̓éməl̓
canoe pole sxʷáq̓ʷən
canoe bailer VU ċéŋtən̓, VU sqʷəlsət, LD θéŋtən̓
  bail (a canoe or boat) VU q̓ʷéləsət, LD q̓ʷéləst
get aboard (canoe, now car, etc.) ʔá·ɬ
pull a canoe up on beach xʷk̓ʷáɬ
white man's boat pút (< English)
oar VU pútəlkʷes, LD pútəl̓kʷes
automobile q̓émqsn̓
streetcar VU kʷələkʷənéŋət, LD kʷələkʷənéŋət ("lot of people running")
he's riding a horse VU sċéʔcə? tə stiqíw, LD sθéʔθə? tə stiqíw
take a shortcut VU q̓émésət

  Food
food sʔíɬən, VU x̣ɬás
provisions, lunch VU séw̓n, LD séw̓n
deer, deer meat smáyis, TB smáyiθ 'meat'
flesh, meat (on ducks/deer) sɬíqʷ
bread VU səplíl, LD səpəlíl (< Chinook Jargon)
  bread dough after it has risen VU spéxʷ səplíl
oil, grease, fat snás
oil (from codfish, seal) snasʔémən
butter VU snəsélŋəxʷ, LD snəséləŋəxʷ
barbecued salmon VU sq̓ʷéləŋ
  to barbecue salmon q̓ʷéləŋ
smoked salmon VU sq̓éylaʔ, LD sq̓éyl·aʔ
  smoking salmon q̓əláʔaŋ
sliced salmon sq̓éləmq̓əm̓ sčé·nəxʷ
  sliced sq̓éləmq̓əm̓
fresh fish soup sɬáp̓ sčé·nəxʷ
fish soup from dried fish sməx̣ʷíɬs
eulachon oil ƛ̓ínə?
barbecued fish head q̓ʷəlíqʷ
whole smoked herring sk̓ʷsím
open smoked herring skʷə́lč
whole smoked fish sx̣éč sčéʔenəxʷ
stink eggs spá?
fish eggs hung in an air bladder šəpəlíwə?
fish eggs in a barrel sƛ̓əm̓k̓ʷ
soft edible bone in fish head sx̣épəkʷ

soup, stew słáp̓

  to eat soup łáp̓

  eating soup/stew/Indian ice-cream VU łáłəp̓, LD łáłp̓

  boiling (anything: soup, water, tide) VU łəp̓áq̓ʷən (q̓ʷ ~ qʷ)

    boiling water VU łəp̓áqʷən qʷá?

roast potatoes (cooked outside in sand) sčénən sqéws ("buried potato")

oven-baked potatoes səqíŋəł sqéws

to bake qkʷéŋ

frying (or poss. 'fry') VU k̓ʷésŋ

  scald it, throw a fish on the fire k̓ʷésət

  put fish or clams on the fire sk̓ʷésəŋ

boil something qʷéləst

barbecue/roast it VU q̓ʷélət

  cooked; ripe VU q̓ʷél

  it's already cooked VU sq̓ʷáłəł

cook it with steam, cook it in a steam-pit VU čénəst, čénəst

tobacco sménəš (cf. 'pitch' under flora above)

to smoke (unclear whether tobacco or fish/meat, prob. both, see 'pipe' and
  'smoking shed') TB pék̓ʷŋ

also see list of flora and fauna above for many things eaten and notes on
  how some are eaten or prepared

Qualities

(all but a few of the words below can appear as cited with a stative
meaning and third person subject as complete sentences or sentence-
initial main verbs; most can also precede nominals directly to
function as adjectives; the few transitive verbs included here cannot
do either)

small VU ƛúƛeʔ, LD ƛúƛaʔ, also VU,TB məmímən 'small, little'

big hayí, TB həyí

hard téqʷ

soft (as of dirt, bed, grass, butter) VU qíʔqaʔ, LD qíʔqə

long, tall (of tree) ƛíqt, TB ƛéqt

  tall (of a person) ƛəqtéʔɫ

short VU čečáyeƛ, LD čəčáẏəƛ, TB čečéẏeƛ

  short (of a person) VU čičəƛéʔɫ

good-looking (of house, road, person, etc.) ʔəẏáẏmət

fat nás (=TB)

skinny (of people) sqʷəqʷə́m̓x̣ʷ

thick (of layer) čɫə́t

thick around (of rope, tree, etc.) mə́qʷ

  thick tree sməqʷíɫč

thin (of layer, as of blanket, canoe) čičəmíyəl ~ (či)čəmíyəl

thin (of rope, tree, etc.) VU x̣ʷíx̣ʷaʔx̣ʷiẏ, LD x̣ʷíʔx̣ʷaʔx̣ʷiẏ, TB x̣ʷíx̣ʷax̣ʷi

wide ɫqə́t

  (he) has a wide nose VU hiyə́qsn

he has a narrow nose VU x̣ʷəx̣ʷiẏə́qsn̓, LD x̣ʷəx̣ʷiẏə́qsn

strong (of a person, of someone's mind, etc.) k̓ʷámk̓ʷəm̓ ~ k̓ʷámk̓ʷəm

strong (of clothing/material) téqʷ

weak (of a person, board) qəqəɫém̓

rotten VU c̓áq̓ʷŋ, LD θáq̓ʷŋ

  rotten tree VU pqʷéẏ, LD pqʷíẏ

far čák̓ʷ, TB léʔel ~ líʔel (VU says líl is 'far' only in Saanich)

near VU stésəɫ, LD stésɫ, TB θíŋəl

dry (fish, land, wood, etc.) x̣éẏčŋ, TB x̣éčəŋ

wet VU c̓ám̓ŋ, LD θám̓ŋ

soaked (of a person) ɫc̓ə́m̓tŋ

  soak something (fish, clothes) VU t̓éləqiʔt, LD t̓éləqit

hot (something touched, weather) k̓ʷéləs (=TB)

lukewarm támʷəl

cold (of weather) VU c̓áɫəŋ, LD θáɫŋ

cold (to touch); pity VU c̓íx̣ʷəŋ, LD,TB θíx̣ʷəŋ

high VU síʔsəɫ, LD síʔsɫ

low VU ƛéčəɫ corrected to ƛéčɫ, LD ƛéčɫ

at the bottom VU ƛíɫəč, LD ƛéɫəč

straight (stick, road, canoe) VU sáq̓ʷəɫ, LD sáq̓ʷɫ

crooked (tree, road, canoe, person, nose) VU sk̓ʷác̓əɫ, LD sk̓ʷáθɫ

real crooked   VU sk̓ʷəlk̓ʷác, LD sk̓ʷəlk̓ʷáθ
old (of tree, person, etc.)   s?éləxʷ, TB ?es?éləxʷ
new, fresh   x̣áẉəs ~ x̣áwəs, TB x̣áẉəs
fast, hurry   x̣ʷə́ŋ
slow   q̓əq̓énəɫ
have a sharp edge   ?áya?s, TB ?áyeθ
  he has a sharp nose   ?iyəsə́qsən, sqə́mqsən
have a dull/blunt edge/point   q̓éla?s, TB q̓él·eθ ~ q̓él·es
sharpen it   šṕə́qst
  have a sharp point, sharp on the end   šṕə́qsəṅ
flatten it   VU čičəmíɫt, LD čičəmí?əlt
shallow (of water)   VU šéšəṁ
deep (of water, hole, cut, spear in animal)   ɫə́č
smooth (of wood)   VU ?ə́ẏ sləq̓íẉs, LD ?ə́ẏ sləq̓íẉs
smooth-splitting   VU ?əẏáləs, LD ?əẏál·əs
rough-splitting (of wood, canoe, post, etc.)   VU x̣əsáləs, LD sx̣əsál·əs
clean (person, clothes, etc.)   VU scéẏcəẇ, LD sééẏθəẇ
dirty (of physical or verbal qualities), ugly   qəlí:ma?, TB q̓ə́ɫəl ~ q̓éləl
  'dirty'
nice, clean (of house)   ?aẏí:ma?
rich; dear; leader, boss, respected person   siẏém
  get rich   VU siẏámsət, LD siẏámst
poor   ləš̓činánət
tight (clothes or in a box)   sčíẉəṗ [sčí?wuṗ]
really tight (of rope, parts in canoe, etc.)   VU stáq̓ʷəɫ, LD stáq̓ʷɫ
loose (of clothes)   sṅáṅəqʷ
full   láθ̓   (rare VU θ̓)
  it is full   VU sléc̓əɫ, LD sléθ̓ɫ
empty (house, bucket)   š̓ɫéṅəɫ
level   sləq̓énəkʷ   ("level ground")
tilted (of house, canoe)   LD təẇíṅ
dead   sq̓ʷáq̓ʷiẏ
alive   helí ~ həlí, TB helí 'to live'
sleepy   ?ətátṅ
asleep   VU náqʷəɫ, LD náqʷɫ
awake   sx̣ʷáẏəɫ
  lively; diligent   sx̣ʷəẏx̣ʷəẏ
a little lazy (temporarily)   séx̣ʷəŋ
  lazy (always)   séx̣ʷsəx̣ʷ
happy   VU s(h)í(?)iləkʷ, LD shí?iləkʷ
sad   sqé?iləs
good   ?ə́ẏ (=TB but TB ~ ?áẏ)
bad   sx̣é?es, TB x̣é?es
it's right, okay   sɫáɫəṁ ~ sɫá?ɫəṁ
right, the correct way, the right thing   TB ?əw sí?it

it's wrong ʔəsʔáy̓q

brave xʷsiy̓áməs

just always afraid (ʔə́w̓) sə́y̓siy̓ ʔəl

generous (with food) xʷʔə́y̓wəɫ

stingy (with food) xʷqə́lwəɫ

generous (with help, money, food) VU xʷəy̓íkʷən, LD xʷiʔíkʷən

hungry k̓ʷéy̓k̓ʷiy̓

full (of stomach), satiated (with food) VU mə́q̓, VU smə́q̓əl

thirsty, want to drink VU qʷaqʷəʔéɬŋən̓, LD qʷaqʷəʔéɬənən̓

sweet VU sáqʷəŋ

it's sour (in taste, like a lemon, berries) VU sáy̓əm

bright, light (inside) sté?təw̓

dark ɬéč

bright colors ʔey̓áləs

white pə́q̓

black nəq̓éx̣ (=TB)

  blackish q̓éx̣əl

  negro VU nəq̓éx̣eyeʔ

green (as grass), yellow, pale (of a person); dark navy blue (not sky blue)(?)

  nəqʷə́y ~ nəqʷə́y̓

red (esp. bright red) nəsə́qʷ (=TB)

  reddish, poss. brown VU k̓ʷíy̓iməl (prob. Saanich)

brown (sic), grey nəxʷík̓ʷ

  whitish grey pq̓áləs nəxʷík̓ʷ

lightweight LD xʷəxʷéw̓xʷə

heavy LD,TB x̣ə́m

easy; cheap LD líɬəq

difficult LD ƛ̓íʔ

  expensive LD ƛ̓íʔtəŋ

raw LD x̣íθ

ripe; cooked q̓ʷə́l

  ripe; cooked VU sq̓ʷáɬəl, LD sq̓ʷáɬ(ə)ɫ

smart, know how to sčuw̓ét

stupid LD sqíʔqəl

sober LD sṗáɬ·

drunk LD sxʷəxʷík̓ʷtŋ

wild tə́ɬtələw̓

tame LD q̓ʷél̓q̓ʷəl̓

stiff all over LD qáɬst

stiff/tight (of knitting) LD t̓qʷáləs

stiff (of denim) LD x̣áq

supple LD mə́t̓mət̓

few TB ʔə́w̓ k̓ʷín̓ ʔaɬ, LD ƛ̓úƛ̓a ʔaɬ

many ŋə́n̓ (=TB)

Verbs Cited (excluding those already listed in classified lists above,
   but including most with new continuative/non-continuative pairs)
A
advise s-o nəpə́t
again, repeat it qəlét ~ qəlét
aim it máčt
   it was aimed smáməytŋ
angry, mad ƚéy̓əq̓
   many are mad/angry ƚəléy̓əq̓
   always mad ƚəƚéy̓əq̓
B
way back/way up on land (away from the water) VU čáɬəqʷ
bail oneself LD qʷéləst
barbecue, roast q̓ʷələŋ
   barbecuing VU q̓ʷələ́ŋ
barking (of a dog) wəwəséɬs
bathe VU šák̓ʷŋ ~ sák̓ʷən
   bathing TB šák̓ʷn̓
   bathe s-o sák̓ʷt
   to swim šišk̓ʷám̓
   swimming šišk̓ʷáʔam̓
   many swimming VU šilišk̓ʷəm̓, LD šilišk̓ʷám̓
believe VU q̓éɬ
blow s-th up (with mouth), blow s-th off VU,TB páxʷət
   the wind spxʷə́laʔ
   blowing (of the wind) VU pəxʷéɬs
play the bone game, play slahal ləhéɬ
   playing slahal ləhéʔeɬ
it's stale, boring VU p̓éxʷəŋ
be born TB kʷín̓
break (of a stick) VU ƚək̓ʷ
   break it (of a stick) tk̓ʷét
   break it accidentally, managed to break it VU tək̓ʷnə́xʷ, LD tək̓ʷnáxʷ
shake it and make it fall, brush s-th off VU píxʷət
   brush oneself off VU pxʷísət, LD pxʷíst
it's burned VU čáqʷəɬ
it burst (of a sore) VU mə́q̓ʷ
C
canoe racing tétəy̓
it can't be, it's impossible VU sk̓ʷéy
(a carved pole sxƚə́k̓ʷŋ)
   carving a pole x̣ə́ƚk̓ʷŋ
change s-th VU ʔəyéqt
   move oneself, get out of the way, go off to one side, dodge s-th
      VU ʔə́čəqsət, LD ʔə́čəqst

come ʔəné, TB ʔəné
  coming ʔiʔəné?ə
come up to the surface (of liquid) VU p̓ékʷŋ
  floating VU p̓əp̓ékʷŋ̓
count s-th k̓ʷsét
  counting s-th k̓ʷə́st
  to count k̓ʷséŋ
  counting k̓ʷésŋ̓
  be counted ʔəsk̓ʷásɬ
to crawl čtéŋ
  crawling čə́tŋ̓
it's going crooked VU yéʔ k̓ʷəćésət
  crooked (of tree, road, canoe, person, etc.) VU sk̓ʷáćɬ, LD sk̓ʷáθ̓ɬ
  real crooked VU sk̓ʷəɫk̓ʷáć, LD sk̓ʷəɫk̓ʷáθ̓
cry, weep x̣ʷáŋ
  crying, weeping x̣ʷəʔáŋ̓
D
different néč
  many different néčnəč
dive néqəŋ
  keep diving repeatedly nəqnéqəŋ
get dressed VU ʔíćəŋ
  getting dressed VU ʔećéŋ̓, LD ʔeθ̓éŋ̓
  dress s-o VU ʔəćéŋəstxʷ, LD ʔəθ̓éŋəstxʷ
  dress s-o (a child) VU ʔəćeŋístxʷ, LD ʔəθ̓eŋístxʷ
drink VU qʷáqʷaqʷəʔ, TB qʷáʔqʷə
drip (once), a drop of water VU ćq̓éŋ, LD θ̓q̓éŋ
  slow dripping VU ćéq̓əŋ̓, LD θ̓éq̓əŋ̓
  dripping lots VU ćəq̓ćéq̓əŋ̓, LD θ̓əq̓θ̓éq̓əŋ̓
(a drum; drumstick q̓áwət)
  drumming q̓awétŋ̓
E
eat VU ʔíɬən
  eating VU ʔíʔɬəŋ̓
eat soup ɬáp̓
  eating soup/stew/Indian ice cream VU ɬáɬəp̓, LD ɬáɬp̓
enter the water TB ʔi(-)q̓énəsət (ŋ̓?)
line it up, make oneself even (of people, canoes, etc.) VU ləq̓ésət
  even VU sléq̓əɬ
F
get fat snás·ət
he's feeding them VU x̣əɫáʔast(ə)s
fight k̓ʷíntəl
  fighting k̓ʷíwəntəl
figure s-th out x̣čə́t

     figur(ing) s-th out (by oneself) x̣ə̇čt
     know s-o VU x̣čít
     learn s-th TB x̣čínəx̣ʷ
fill s-th VU ləċə́t
     it is full VU sléċəɫ, LD sléθ̇ɫ
finish VU háy
fish for herring (to rake) ɫéṫəṁ (m ?)
     fishing for herring ɫéṫəṁ
flow TB ṗkʷétŋ
G
gather q̇ə́p
     many are gathered VU sq̇əlq̇ə́p
     be gathered VU sq̇épəɫ
get in a canoe, get in (canoe, car, etc.), get aboard ʔá·ɫ
     getting in (canoe, car, etc.) VU ʔáʔaləɫ, LD ʔáʔaɫɫ
give it to s-o VU ʔəŋá̇ʔt
     given TB ʔáŋəstəŋ
     supplying s-th TB ʔəŋáʔsé̇ʔt
go, go to, going (to) yé̇ʔ
go through a narrow place (in mountains/crowd) VU x̣ʷə̇čə́sət, LD x̣ʷə̇čə́st
go toward, come toward VU híẇəɫ, LD híẇəl
go up (a hill) VU sáŋ
grab s-th kʷə́nət
     get s-th (a cold for ex.) VU kʷə́n·əx̣ʷ
     taking it, holding it kʷənét
     take it (be taken?) kʷənésəŋ
     taking it (being taken?) kʷəṅésəŋ
     I was held by s-o TB kʷikʷəṅtíŋələsən
growing up TB čísəŋ
H
hatch; get sober, come to one's senses ṗə́ɫ
     be sober LD sṗáɫ·
     a lot hatched ṗəɫṗə́ɫ
     a lot hatched ṗəɫṗə́ɫə̇čɫ ~ LD ṗəɫṗɫíkʷs
help s-o (take pity on s-o) VU ċəx̣ʷíŋət
they're helping each other VU kʷənəŋítəɫ (cf. 'run'?)
be here ʔéɫe ~ ʔéɫaʔ ~ ʔéɫəʔ
get here VU téčəl
hide VU kʷé·l
got hit (by s-th in air, ground or water) VU ċə́s
     got hit (by s-th thrown) by s-o VU ċsə́təŋ
     getting hit VU ċə́stəŋ
     hit s-th (accidentally, by throwing) VU ċə́snəx̣ʷ
     s-o was hit in the face x̣ʷċsástŋ̇
     many were hit in the face θ̇əl̇əsástŋ̇

hit s-th tíqʷənəxʷ
  tíʔqʷət hitting s-th
make a hole in s-th sɬə́qʷt
  get a hole in it VU səɬqʷáẁəč
holler, yell; to phone kʷéčŋ
  hollering VU kʷəkʷéčŋ
  holler at s-o; phone s-o kʷəčéŋət
how many is it? k̓ʷín
  how many people is it? k̓ʷənélə
get hurt VU méʔkʷəɬ, LD méʔkʷɬ
  many got hurt məméʔkʷɬ
  get hurt over and over LD mélə̓kʷɬ

I
insult s-o regarding his body psə́qʷt
  insulting s-o regarding his body pə́sqʷt

J
jump xʷítŋ

K
know s-o (see 'figure out' above)
he knows (how to do) it sčə̓wét

L
laugh nə́čəŋ
  laughing nənə́yəŋ̓
  s-o is being laughed at over and over nəlnəčátəŋ̓
leave s-o alone VU kʷéʔet
lie (tell a made-up story) TB qéyəxqən
  telling a made-up story VU xʷqéyəxqəŋ̓, LD (correcting) qeyəxqénəŋ̓
lying down səsé̓wt
line them up, pile them up VU t̓ə́ŋ̓ət
  all lined up VU stén̓əɬ
lock s-th VU xʷləkəlít

M
mean to, intention slə́l (nominal used as verb like sx̌íʔ 'want, like')
to melt VU čáx̌ʷən
miss it, move it VU qʷíx̌ʷət, LD qʷíx̌ʷt
  miss it (accidentally) qʷíx̌ʷnəxʷ
make a mistake míləčəs
  be making a mistake ʔesmíʔiləčəs

N
get near, approach VU tə́s
  be near VU stésəɬ, LD stésɬ
no, not to be, is not ʔə́wə ~ ʔáwə (ʔáwə less common)
  it is nothing, it is none, it is nobody ʔə́wənə

O
be outside ʔəséqɬ

go outside sqílŋ

P

patch s-th (canoe, clothes, ceiling, anything) xʷq̓pə́t
  patching s-th xʷq̓ə́pt
  patching q̓p̓éls
it peeled off (bark for ex.), came off (of s-th stuck on) VU ɫə́q̓ʷ
poison s-o VU c̓əxtənít, LD θ̓əxtənít
poor (in wealth/spirits) tsás
push/shove s-o/s-th sx̌ə́t (=TB)
  pushing it sə́xt
put s-th down VU sékʷəs, LD sékʷs
  putting s-th down se?éẃəs
put it in the sack VU lisékt
put out a fire ƛ̓ə́k̓ʷəla?
  putting out a fire ƛ̓k̓ʷéls
Q
R
rain VU ɫə́məxʷ
  raining VU ɫə́m̓xʷ
rested qík̓ʷəŋ
  be resting sqí?qəẃ
getting rich VU siẏ́ámsət, LD siẏ́ámst
  brave xʷsiẏ́ám̓əs
run VU kʷániŋət
  run after s-o kʷəŋŋátnəs
run away ƛ̓íẃ
S
same as, kind of TB xʷəńéŋ
get scared, fear, be afraid of séẏsiẏ̓ (=TB)
  scare oneself VU seẏ́siẏ̓náŋət
scatter s-th ƛ̓pə́xt
  he/she is scattering s-th VU ƛ̓ə́pxtəs, LD ƛ̓ə́pxts
  scattering ƛ̓píxəŋ̓
scratch it (on purpose) VU x̌íčət
see s-o VU léŋnəxʷ
  look at s-o VU léŋət
  watching it ləŋít
  take care of oneself (watch oneself) VU leŋásət, LD leŋást
  tak(ing) care of oneself leŋəsát
shaking qʷə́ẏəxəŋ̓
have a sharp nose sqə́mqsən
sharpen it VU šípət, LD šípt
sharpening s-th t̓əqá?st
to shiver ɫtə́xtŋ
  shivering ɫə́txtŋ

show off LD čákʷəsət, VU čə́kʷəsət
  showing off čáẁst
sing VU,TB t́íləm
  singing LD t́íləm̀, VU t́ət́íləm̀
  lots singing t́əĺíləm
sit, sit down, sit up VU ʔə́mət
  sitting down, etc. VU ʔámət
  little child sitting (up/down), sitting by oneself lonely VU ʔaʔámət
  seat s-o VU ʔəmáttxʷ
sleep VU ʔítət, LD ʔítt
  sleeping LD ʔíʔtt
  sleepy ʔətátǹ
it got smashed VU t́əs
  break it (dishes, window, door, canoe) t́sə́t
  break it accidentally t́əsnáxʷ
smelled s-th háqʷnəxʷ
  smelling s-th háʔqʷnəxʷ
snow falls číq
  snow is falling VU čéyəq
spilled (of a container) VU kʷə́l̇
  spill, tip (oneself over) in a canoe, overturn, capsize VU kʷə́ləsət,
  LD kʷə́ləst
spit čx̣ʷál̇s
  spitting čx̣ʷáʔl̇s
splash s-o ł̇əltást
  splashing s-o ł̇əl̇tást
split it, tear it čx̣ə́t
  tearing it, splitting it (canoe with wedge for ex.) čə́x̣t
  split it by accident, happened to split it, (finally) managed to split it
  čəx̣náxʷ
  split it (of a head) čx̣íqʷt
  splitting wood VU čx̣áləẁsaʔ, LD čx̣áləẁs(ə)
stand síl̇əǹ
  standing səsíl̇əǹ
steal qéǹ
  stealing qéqəǹ
get stuck (like clothes in chair, etc.) k̇ə́q̇ʷ
surprised VU čə́q̇
sweat VU čáq̇ʷŋ
  sweating VU čáq̇ʷǹ

T

being taken toward VU tx̌ənétəǹ
talk, speak, say VU qʷél
  talking qʷáqʷəl̇
  giving a speech qʷəqʷél̇

talk too much qʷə́lqʷəl
  talking (too much) VU qʷə́lqʷəɫ
  thoughts, feelings šqʷəlqʷəléwəṅ ("nom.-habitual-talk-in the mind")
be there lé?e
from there, from where? VU čsəlé?e
get tight VU tə́qʷ
train (dancing, sport, canoe-pulling, etc.) VU ɫéy̓əsət
  training VU ɫéy̓ɫəsət
he was tripped ɫəkʷšə́ṅətəṅ
true, truly si?ít
turn oneself over VU čə́ləw̓sət, LD čə́ləw̓st
U
understand (it) VU təɫnáṅət
use s-th čák̓ʷs
  using s-th ča?áw̓əs
V
W
wake s-o up xʷčə́t
  waking s-o up xʷə́y̓t
  awake sxʷáy̓əɫ
walk VU štə́ṅ
  walking VU šə́təṅ
  taking a little walk šəšə́təṅ
  he's walking around VU šəštəṅásəṅ
want, like sx̌í? (=TB) (a nominal but possessed with no preceding article
  and used as a verb)
getting warmer VU k̓ʷés·ət
wash it VU c̓ék̓ʷt
get wet VU c̓əmáṅəsət ~ θ̓əmáṅəsət
what is it? VU stéṅ
  what is it being? stéṅ (as in VU stéṅ kʷənə šqʷəlqʷəléwəṅ 'What am I
    thinking?', LD stéṅ kʷəṅ šqʷəlqʷəléwəṅ 'What are you thinking?' lit.
    "What is it being? + your + thoughts")
  what color is it? steṅáləs
what did s-o say? ?íṅət
where is he from? VU čsəlé?es
he's whistling šəšpəlás
who is it? VU wét
have a wide nose hiyə́qsn (√'big')
wish for s-th/s-o VU štíṅət
used to get wood TB sčiy̓áɫələ
working VU čé?e
write it x̌ə́ɫət
  writing it x̌ə́ɫt
  get it written down sx̌éɫəɫstəxʷ

```
   writing (?)   x̣ə́ɫəlaʔ
   he's a writer   x̣əɫéɫs
X
Y
yell   (see 'holler')
Z
```

5. THE STORY OF qʷəlásəlwət, MAIDEN OF DECEPTION PASS

5.1. Short English Version, told by Victor Underwood, July 11, 1984
  (Tape #1) before telling the story in Samish

   Well, the way the old people used to tell me, you know, they lived
right there, you know, at Deception Pass. They lived there for fish-
ings and all that stuff. They had a place, a whole village there.
And she used to go down, down to the beach, alone. And that's when
this man come up, come up to get her. Because when she did go down
below-, She went down below; they took her down there, and it was
just like this; you can see the village. There was a village. You
can see all their people. Didn't bother her any. And she stayed
there and she come back up.

   This man was a monster, went right up, asked their [her] parents--
I'm just cutting it short, you know--asked her-, asked their [her]
parents if they [he and his people] could take her down. Parents says
"No." They can feel everything got cold in the house, you know, got
cold when he was coming up. You know, he's from down in the sea.
When he got up there and he asked and they says [that], and he says,
"Well, if you don't let me have your daughter," he says, "we'll
starve you people." He says, "I'm the king, king of the sea."
Well that's the way-, close as I can say in English, "I'm the king
of the sea, down there." But ʔésə siyéms tə ƛíƛəč tə sʔiłən
['I am the chief/head-man of the food down below.']. That means,
well, as close as I can say it, 'king of the sea.' "I supply all
the food, you know, everything down below. If you don't give me
your daughter you people will starve; everything will go."

   Well they answered him that he took their daughter away, people
will get a lot of fish, everything they need, everything they eat
from the sea. They can get it anytime, anytime, you see. And
barnacles and mussels, anything that they can eat down at the sea,
they have it. And this guy done it for oh, quite a while; I don't
know how long it is.

   And when she comes and visits her parents, well she comes by
herself, and soon the barnacles start to grow, you know, a barnacle
on her face, [sea]weeds. Her parents says, "You better not come up
no more." That's why you see that, how they got that barnacle [on
her face on the totem pole carving at Deception Pass]. It was real-,
I don't have to tell them when they called me; they [the carvers]
had everything, everything, you know. Well them days I didn't care;
I should have taken it all in, but I never know I was going to be

telling people, you know."

5.2. Longer English Version, told by Victor Underwood, July 11, 1984 (Tape #1), after telling the story in Samish.

As I say, Samish was the biggest tribe, you know. It's the biggest tribe they ever had that I was told. I was told by my grandfather. It was the biggest tribe. They had houses, houses all around, that's in Guemes. And I seen-, I lived in Guemes when I was a kid. But I seen the poles but I never seen the houses. And the Samish used to be together all the time.

And they went to Deception Pass, that's where their fishing grounds was. There was a big village there; they stayed right there. They do a lot of fishing. Everything is what they eat from the sea, everything they want; they had everything there, mussels and all that, everything of sea-food they can eat. They have always had it there.

One day this girl, daughter of this- one of the old people, went down the beach. She would stay down on the beach for-, goes down every day. Every day she goes down there. Pretty soon she went down the beach and went into the water, washing. Somebody grabbed her and [s]he looked and it was a hands. So they dragged her down, dragged her down the beach, down under the water. When she got down there she felt the water when she was going, but after she got down it was just like the way we are now, you see. She looked back and seen all her people, seen the village; everything was, you know, it was just the same as we are today. So this man told her—he was a nice looking man—"I been watching you. I been watching you every day when you come down. And I had kind of worked on you so you can come down." Well them days people used to work on somebody that they want to get ahold of. They work on them. I wouldn't know how to say it, but the Indians had their own way. They had their own power. If they want anybody, well, they work on it so they can come down. So they talked and [he] says, "Well I want to marry you. So I'm going to go up and ask your parents if you can, you can come down with me."

So they went up. They got up and people were kind of worried about their daughter and can feel that cold cold in the house before he walked in. He walked in and they seen him, a good-looking man, and he talked to the parents. He says, "I had your daughter down below." He says, "I'm the king of the sea." He says, "I'm the king [of] everything that you eat, everything, the fish, everything that you got down below to eat." And he says, "I look after it. I'm the king. And if you don't let me have your daughter," he says, "your people

are going to starve. You wouldn't get nothing out of me. [There'll]
be no fish or anything that you eat." So they talked it over and says,
"Well yeah, I guess you can go."

So they took her daughter down, and she comes up to see their parents.
They done that for I wouldn't know how long. It just took quite a while,
in a way to go down, up, up and see their parents. Pretty soon the
barnacles started to grow, the weeds started to grow on her thigh. So
the old man says, "You better not come back." He says, "We're okay.
You say you can see us, so we're all fine here." He says [that] to her
because she felt bad her daughter was turning to sea, like. That's why
they told her not to come back.

So Samish had lots to eat, everything they need; everything they need
they go get out, even after, after-time people, Samish, used to over and
call her name, "qʷəlásəɬwət, we want something to eat." They čí·tən,
'thanked her', when I want something that's going to come we need.
Now the Samish people never starve; they get all the food they want.
They go out and get it. Even if they're travelling through there's
supposed to have been real swift water, and they talk to her, kind of
talk to her that they're from the tribe. The water settles down; they
can go right up with their canoe. No trouble at all because they
believed her, she's down there. They called her name. That's how
people used to go. That's all far as I can remember. Yeah.

5.3. Samish version, told by Victor Underwood, July 11, 1984 (tape #1)

Each line of Samish is numbered and is followed by five lettered
lines for corrections and analysis which Victor gave on June 29, 1985
(Tapes 55, 56, and 57). Line a is for alternate Samish words usually to
replace Saanich forms given in error in the original telling (Saanich
forms are preceded by a right parenthesis) or sometimes just to improve
on the Samish word choice given above it. Line m is for segmented
morphological analysis (where known). Line s is for syntactic analysis.
Lines m and s were not given by Victor but done later. Line w is for a
word-by-word translation. Line f is for fluent English translation of each
sentence. More work remains to be done on this text, further morphological and syntactic analysis, better glosses for a few words, and
analysis into acts, scenes, and stanzas, all structured by stylistic
features of particles, conjunctions, repetitions, and content (analysis
as proposed in Hymes 1981 and elsewhere). The speech by TB and the
stories by LD remain to be completely transcribed and analyzed as well.
It would be premature to analyze this story as to style without doing
some of that homework first.

Abbreviations for lines m and s:

= derivational affix

- inflectional affix

-X- inflectional infix X

$C_1 \partial C_2$- prefixed reduplication type (for ex. used for 'plural')

$-C_1 \partial C_2$ suffixed reduplication type (for ex. 'habitual')

(-)?V_1?- (infixed?) irregular plural reduplication found in some roots /#s_iy
  (if the #s is a prefix, the reduplication is a prefix, if #s is part of the
  root, the reduplication would be an infix; this type found also in Halkomelem)

1s   1st person singular

1p   1st person plural

2   2nd person

2p   2nd person pluralizer

3   3rd person

apos   apposition

art   demonstrative article

caus   'causative' control transitivizer

cjec   'conjectural' particle

conj   conjunction

ctras   'contrastive to preceding information' particle

ctv   continuative aspect

dem   demonstrative

demadv   demonstrative adverb

dim   diminutive

distal   'invisible, remote, abstract, indefinite' demonstrative form

dur   durative aspect

eff   effort transitivizer

evid   'evidential' particle

expl   'explanative' particle

fem   'female' demonstrative

fut   future tense

hab   'habitual' aspect

impt   imperative (sometimes vt-obj with no subject pronoun = imperative)

incep   'inceptive' -sət ('get, become, turn')

indef   indefinite

ipron   independent pronoun

mid   middle voice

motion-   prefix indicating 'in motion, travelling while'

nc   non-control transitivizer

nom   nominal

nom-, -nom   nominalizer

nom as v   nominal used as verb (in syntactic verb position)

NP   nominal phrase

nrbeg   narrative beginning (oddly enough, háy 'finish' is used to show
    this; this use is stated by VU and found in both texts by him and TB)

nrend   narrative ending (ʔəsə́p is used to show this)

obj   object

obl   oblique case

pass   passive voice

past   past tense

pcl   particle

-pcl   usually particle ʔəẃ when it takes forms without ʔ and is phonologically
  attached to the preceding word

persis   'persistent' aspect

pl   plural

presum   'presumptive' particle

pron   pronoun

prox   proximal demonstrative

psv   possessive pronoun form

pur   purposeful control transitivizer

recip   reciprocal

refl   reflexive

req   'request information' particle

res   resultive aspect

rlcl   relative clause

sbj   subject

stat   stative aspect

subcl   subordinate clause

subsbj   subordinate subject pronoun affix

v   verb

vadj   adjectival verb

vadv   adverbial verb

vaux   auxiliary verb

vdem   demonstrative verb

vi   intransitive verb

vneg   negative verb

voc   vocative (nominal used as term of address with no article preceding)

vprep   prepositional verb

Vpron   pronominal verb/verbal pronoun

Vq   interrogative verb

vt   transitive verb

The Story of qʷəláŵsəlwət, Maiden of Deception Pass

```
1. sinémiš      tə      sʔəẉ    háy     )čə́q    )xʷílŋəxʷ,      síẏém
a. sʔémiš                       həyí    ʔəɫtélŋəxʷ              sʔíʔiẏem
m.             dem     nom-ctras nrbeg                          -ʔVₗʔ- pl
s. nom as v    art     pcl     vadv    vadj    nom     sbj     vadj
w. is Samish   the     then    real    big     people/tribe    well-respected
f. The biggest people/tribe then were the Samish, well-respected


2. )xʷílŋəxʷ.   )čə́q.   níɫ     su      lé·s    ʔáẉ     kʷsu    ʔálməts
a. ʔəɫtélŋəxʷ   həyí                             ʔáwə
m.                     pro/dem nom-ctras -3sbj  vneg    kʷ-s-ʔəẉ -l- pl?
s. nom sbj      vadj    conjunction vdem    vi      dem-ctras vi-3sbj
w. people/tribe be big they    so      they're it's not that    they're
w.                             there                           sitting
f. people. They're big. So they're there; those that go aren't just


3. ʔəɫ     tə      yéʔ.    ʔáx̣ʷ    ʔə      tə      šxʷʔáx̣ʷs   čé·nəxʷ.
a.                                         kʷ
m.         dem                     dem     nom-vi-3sbj
s. pcl     rlcl    vi      vi      obl     rlcl    vaux       vi
w. just    those who  go    go to          the     where they  to fish
w.                                         distal  go to
f. sitting around home. They go to a place where they go to fish.


4. ƛ̓əléʔeŋ    kʷsəs    ʔíɫəns   tə      scé·nəxʷ.    niɫsu    tás
a.
m. ctv        dem-nom-3psv -3sbj  dem     nom-         dem-ctras
s. vi         subcl    vi/vt?   art     nom obj      conj     vi
w. looking for that they  they eat  the     fish         therefore  get to
w.                                                        they
f. They're looking to eat fish. So they get to/arrive at


5. ʔə      cə      šxʷʔáx̣ʷs.    niɫsu    léʔesələʔ    čéʔeys.     mə́kʷəẉ
a.
m.         dem     nom-  -3sbj          vdem-3sbj-past ctv-3sbj    -ctras
s. obl     rlcl    v as nom     conj    dem          vi          nom as v
w. obl.    the     place where  so      that's where  working     all of them
w.                 they're going        they were
f. the place where they're going. So that's where they were working. All


6. sƛ̓íʔs    kʷs     kʷə́n·əxʷs   kʷ      sʔíɫəns   tə      sƛ̓əlíƛ̣qəɫ.
a.
m. -3psv   dem-nom  -nc-3sbj    dem     nom-  -3psv dem     -əl- pl
s. nom as v subcl   vt          distal  nom obj      art     nom
```

w. they want that   they get it some   their food/ the   children
w.   food of
f. of them want to get some food for the children.

7. níɫsu   lé?es   cəẁ   nəní?ɫiye?   )xʷílŋəxʷ   sq̓épəɫ.
a.   ?əɫtélŋəxʷ   or sq̓əlq̓ép
m.   -3sbj   dem-ctras   stat- + -dur/-pl-
s. conj   vdem   art   pron/dem   nom sbj   vadj
w. so   they're   them   people   gathered
w.   there
f. So those people are gathered there.

8. kʷə́n·əxʷəs   tə   sčé·nəxʷ   ?əẁ   stéŋ   ?əɫ   cəẁ
a.
m.   -nc-3sbj   dem   ctras   dem-ctras
s.   vt   art   nom obj   pcl   vq   pcl   rlcl
w. they get it   the   fish   what   just
w.   =anything
f. They get the fish, anything,

9. mə́kʷstéŋ   ƛ̓íƛəč   ?éɫé   )kʷsə   ƛ̓íƛəč   s?íɫən.
a.
m. vadj=vq   dem
m. or 2 words   prox
s. indef nom   vadj   demadv   art   vadj   nom obj
w. everything   (sea)bottom right here the   (sea)bottom food
f. everything [on the] sea-bottom right here, the sea-bottom food.

10. ?ə́wə   kʷs   níɫ   sk̓ʷéy   cə   sine?émiš-,   sémiš.
a.   s?émiš
m. vneg   dem-nom dem   stat-   dem
s. vi   subcl   pron   vi   art   nom sbj
w. it's not that   they   get hungry the   (error)   Samish
f. The Samish never get hungry.

11. yásələẁ   kʷín·əs   tə   s?íɫəns   txʷíwəɫ   ?ə   tə
a. yás?aləẁ
m. vadv-pcl-ctras -eff-sbj dem   -3psv   txʷ=   dem
s. vadv   vt   art   nom obj   vprep   obl   art
w. always   they get it the their food going to   the
f. They always get their food for

12. sƛ̓əlíƛ̓qəɫs.   níɫsu   kʷə́nəŋs tə-   )k̓ʷən·əxʷs   )kʷsə
a.   (corrected to)   léŋnəxʷs
m. -pl- -3psv   dem-ctras   -nc-(3obj/)-3sbj dem

```
s. nom obj         conj                              vt           prox
w. their children  so then                    she sees it   the/a
f. their children.  So then she saw a
```

13.
```
13. sќɛ́ləqəm    ʔɛ́ɬɛ́      kʷs    yiќíќəč.        štɛ́ŋətəs    sə    sɬɛ́nəẏ.
a.                                  ʔiʔeќíќəč
m.                          dem-nom  motion-      -pur- -3sbj  dem
s. nom obj      demadv    subcl    vadv            vt          art   nom obj
w. powerful     right     that's   down on the    he wished   the   woman
w. monster      here               (sea)bottom    for her     fem.
f. powerful monster right here on the sea bottom.  He wished for the woman
```

14.
```
14. níɬsu      yɛ́ʔs      qsə́sət;     sák̓ʷəŋ.    su     kʷənítəŋs.      su     yɛ́ʔs
a.
m.             -3sbj     -purrefl    -mid       ctras  -pur-persis-pass       -3sbj
s. conj        vaux      vt          vi         conj?  v-3subsbj?      ctras  vaux
w. so          she went  went into   she bathes so     she was        so     he went
w.                       water                         grabbed
f. so she went into the water to bathe.  So she was grabbed.  So he went
```

15.
```
15. yɛ́ʔtəŋ,    ʔáx̣ʷtəŋs    ʔə    kʷs    ʔiyeќíќəč.    sќíʔs      kʷs
a.
m. -pur-pass   -pur-pass          dem    motion-      -3psv      dem
s. vt          vt-3subsbj   obl   rlcl   Vadv         nom as v   subcl
w. she was     she was                   down at the  he wants   that he
w. taken       put there                 (sea)bottom
f. taking her down to put her at the sea bottom.  He wanted to
```

16.
```
16. čtáləs     ʔə     sə     sɬɛ́nəẏ    čəʔɛ́ɬeʔ     ʔə     tə     sq̓ʷíq̓ʷəŋ.
a.
m. č=                dem              čə=                dem    nom/stat-
s. vi         obl    art    nom obj   demadv      obl    art    nom?
w. get a             the    woman     from here          the    out of the
w. spouse            fem.                                       water
f. get as a spouse a woman from here, out of the water.
```

17.
```
17. níɬsu     yɛ́ʔs     ʔáx̣ʷ    ʔə    tə    sʔəɬɛ́ləx̣ʷs.     su    čtɛ́ŋs-,
a.
m.           -3sbj                   dem   -pl-  -3psv     ctras -3sbj
s. conj      vaux     vi       obl   art   nom             conj  vi
w. so        he went  to go          the   her parents     so    he asked-,
f. So he went to go to her parents.  Then he asked-,
```

18.
```
18. čtɛ́ŋ     "nə     sќíʔ     kʷənəs     čtáləs     ʔə     sən̓     ŋɛ́nəʔ.
a.
```

m. -res   1spsv   dem-1spsv-nom č=   dem-2psv

s. vi   pron nom as v subcl   vi   obl art-pron nom obj

w. he asked   it's my want   that I   take as   your   offspring

w.   spouse   fem.

f. he asked, "I want to take your daughter as my wife.

19. ʔə́y̓   sƛíƛəƛqəƛ."   su   qʷéls   sə   sʔéləxʷ,   "ʔáwə

a.   sʔéləxʷ,

m.   ctras -3sbj   dem   vneg

s. vadj   nom   conj   vi   art   nom subj   vi

w. (she) is   child   so she said   the   parent   is not

w. good   fem.

f. She is a good child."   So the mother said, "I don't

20. nə   sƛíʔ   kʷs   yéʔs   sənə   ŋə́nəʔ.   ʔən   sƛíʔ   kʷsu

a.

m. 1spsv   dem-nom   -3sbj dem-1spsv   1spsv   dem-nom-pcl

s.pron nom as v subcl   vi   dem-pron nom sbj pron nom as v subcl

w. my   want   that   she go   my fem. offspring it's want   that

w.   she   my

f. want my daughter to go.   I want

21. ʔéƛes   ʔə   ƛníŋəƛ."   su   qʷéls   tə   sƛéləqəm   čéƛe

a.   čeʔéƛe

m. -3sbj   1p ipron   ctras   -3sbj   dem   čə=

s. vdem   obl   pron   conj   vi   art   nom sbj vadv

w. she's   obl.   us   he talked/ the   monster   from here

w. here   (with)   said

f. her here with us."   So the monster from here

22.)kʷsə   ƛíƛəč,   "nə   sƛíʔ   kʷənə   kʷə́n·əxʷ   sən̓   ŋə́nəʔ.

a.

m. dem   1spsv   dem-1spsv   -nc-3obj   dem-2psv

s. subcl   vadv   pron nom as v subcl-sbj   vt   dem-pron nom obj

w. the   (sea)bottom/ it's want   that I   get/take her   your   offspring

w.   deep   my   fem.

f. on the sea bottom said, "I want to take your daughter.

```
23. há? sʔisxʷ      ʔə́wə     sʔánəs        ʔə   sə̀n    ŋə́nəʔ    ʔi
 a.
 m.       -2sbj     vneg     nom- -1sobjpur     dem-2psv
 s.conj/pcl        vi       subvt          obl  dem-pron nom obj  conj
 w. if you         don't    give me        obl. your    offspring then/
 w.                                             fem.             and
 f. If you don't give me your daughter, then


24. sk̓ʷé·ysəʔ      k̓ʷə̀n    skʷə́n·əxʷ      kʷ   sʔíɬən    čéɬe      kʷs
 a.
 m.        -fut    dem-2psv nom- -nc-3obj  dem            čə=       dem-nom
 s. nom as v       subcl    vt             distal nom obj vadv      subcl
 w. it will be     that you get it         some   food   from here that's
 w.  impossible
 f. it will be impossible for you to get any food from here


25. yiλíλəč      tə      ʔəwmə́kʷsteŋ.  ʔə́sə   siyéms     kʷs   yiλíλəč
 a.                                                              ʔiʔeλíλəč
 m. motion-      dem     pcl?-Vadj=vq  1s ipron   -3psv  dem-nom motion-
 s.  vadv        art     indef nom     vpron   nom apos   rlcl  vadv
 w. down on the  the     everything    I am    chief/leader/ what's on the
 w.  bottom                                    king of               bottom
 f. down on the bottom, everything.  I am the king of what's on the bottom


26. ʔéɬe      kʷs      q̓ʷɬéy̓ənə̀ŋ.   ʔə́sə        ʔəŋá?sé?tsən     ʔṅ
 a.
 m. dem       dem-nom  -1ssubsbj?-?  1s ipron   -pur-ctv-res-1ssbj  -2spsv
 s. vadv      rlcl     v             vpron          vt              pron
 w. here      where I am (?)  I am the one     supplying it      your
 f. here where I am.  I am the one supplying you


27. sʔíɬənhéla.    há?     sə?    skʷə́če    ʔáwə    sʔánəs     ʔə   sṅ
 a.
 m.       -2p      fut     expl   vneg nom-v-pur-1sobj  dem-2psv
 s. nom obj        conj/pcl? pcl  pcl   vi     subvt     obl dem-pron
 w. you folks'     if      fut.         don't  give me           your
 w.  food
 f. folks's food.  If you won't give me your


28. ŋə́nəʔ      ʔi    niɬsʔisu    k̓ʷéyk̓ʷiy̓.   su    mə́k̓ʷ    šxʷə̀né̇ŋs
 a.                               k̓ʷéləy̓
 m.        -fut-nom-ctras  hab =C₁əC₂  ctras         nom- -3sbj
 m.                        or -pl-
 s. nom      conj dem/pron     vi      conj  vadj        vi
 w. offspring then  so fut    (lots) are   so    all    they are the same
```

w.   therefore   hungry
f. daughter, then therefore lots will be hungry.

29. tən   )xʷílŋəxʷ."   niɫsu   xʷtélqəns   ce   čkʷéʔs   ŋə́nəʔ.
a.   ɫtélŋəxʷ
m.   -2psv   -3sbj   dem č=
s.   art-pron nom sbj   conj   vi   art   pron   nom
w.   your   people   and so they answer for   their own   offspring
f. Your people will be all the same." And so they answer for their own
f. daughter.

30. su   yéʔtəŋ   sə   ŋə́nəʔs.   niɫsu   kʷə́n·əxʷs   cəw   mə́kʷsəs
a.
m.   ctras -pur-pass dem   -3psv   -nc-3obj-3sbj dem-pcl? -?
s.   conj   vt   art   nom obj   conj   vt   art   vadj
w.   so   she was   the   their   and then they got it   the   everybody
w.   taken away   fem.   offspring   /all
f. So their daughter was taken away. And then all

31. scélečəs   tə   sʔíɫən   líɫəq.   líɫəq   ʔəl   kʷs
a.   scéleʔčəs
m.   -pl- -3psv dem   pcl   dem-nom
s.   nom sbj   art   nom obj   vadv   vadv   pcl   subcl
w.   their many the   food   easy   it was   just   that they
w.   relatives   easy
f. their many relatives got the food easily. It was just easy for them to

32. kʷə́n·əxʷs   tə   sʔíɫən   čéyɫe   kʷə   ƛíƛəč.   su   wənés
a.   čsəléʔe kʷs ʔiʔəƛíƛəč
m.   -nc-3obj-3sbj dem   č=dem/vi dem   /motion-   ctras when-
m.   -3sbj
s.   vt   art   nom obj vadv/indef subcl   vadv   conj   vaux/vi
w.   they got it the   food   from down that's at the   so   when
w.   there   bottom   she comes
f. get the food from down there at the bottom. So when

33. qʷíqʷən   néw   q̇ʷín   sə   ŋə́nəʔs   )k̇ʷə́ntəŋ   cəw   nəníʔɫiyε.
a.   leŋétəs
m.   vaux-ctras?   dem   -3psv   -pur-3obj-3sbj dem pl=
s.   vadv/vi   vaux-pcl   vi   art   nom sbj   vt   art-ctras pron
w.   (comes) up comes (she comes) the   their   she saw them   them
w.   up out of the fem.   offspring
w.   water
f. their daughter comes up out of the water she saw them.

34. yás   ʔaɫ   tə wənéčiyəxʷ   yu   kʷɫiyú   q̓ʷiq̓ʷəŋ   sə
a.   wə-əné čə yəxʷ   ʔi-əw̓
m.   dem when-come evid cjec conj-pcl pcl-ctras   dem
s. vadv   pcl   subcl?   vi   pcl pcl   conj   pcl   vi   art
w. it's   just   when she's it must be   then   already   comes up   the
w. always   ready   out of the fem.
w.   water
f. Whenever their daughter is ready to come up out of the water

35. ŋénəʔs   yuw   ċɫáŋəsət   tə   snáwəɫ.   ċɫáŋəsət
a.   ċíxʷəŋ   ċíxʷəŋ
m. -3sbj   conj-ctras -res-mid-incep/   dem   stat- -dur
m.   -mid (line a)
s. nom sbj   conj   vi   relcl vi   vi
w. their   it gets cold   the   inside   it gets cold
w. offspring
f. it gets cold inside. It gets cold

36. yuw   kʷɫu   níɫsu   ʔə   x̌číts   tə   skʷéʔs   sʔəléləxʷ.
a. ʔi-əw̓   kʷɫəw   níɫsəw
m. conj-pcl pcl-pcl dem-ctras   -res-pur dem   emph-3psv C₁əC₁- pl
m.   -3obj-3sbj
s. conj   pcl   dem   obl?   vt   art   pron   nom sbj
w. then   already therefore   they   the   her own   parents
w.   know it
f. then therefore her own parents know it.

37. "ʔéɫe   yéxʷ   kʷɫ   ʔiʔenéʔe   kʷsə   siyém   nə   ŋénəʔ.
a.
m.   moving- -ctv   distal   1spsv
s. vdem   pcl   pcl   vi   dem   vadj   pron   nom sbj
w. here   must be   coming   the   dear   my   offspring
w.   fem
f. "My dear daughter (not visible yet or distant) must be coming here.

38. tés,   ʔəw̓   síʔit."   ʔi   )ɫkʷén·əs   tə   skʷéqəq   číʔsəŋ
a.   léŋnəs
m.   ctras   -nc-3obj-3sbj dem   -ctv-mid
s. vi   pcl   vadj   conj   vt   art   nom obj   vi, apos
s.   or new sent.
w. she got really it's true and   he saw it   the   green sea- growing
w. here   weed
f. She got here, it's really true." And he saw green seaweed growing

39. ʔə   tə   sʔásəs·.   níɫ   číʔsəŋ   ʔəné?   məkʷstén.

```
a.
m.        dem      -3psv          -ctv-mid   -ctv?      vadj=vi
s.   obl  art      nom    vdem    vi         vi,apos?   vadj as nom
w.   from the      her face  that's   growing    coming     everything
w.                           the one
f.   from her face.  Everything was growing, coming.


40. ʔənéw̓      čísəŋ     ʔə    tə    sʔásəs.              su    qʷéls
a.                                           ɫéw̓qəm̓.
m.       -ctras   -ctv-mid        dem    -3psv                 ctras  -3sbj
s.   vaux         vi         obl  art    nom         nom        conj   vi
w.   coming out   growing    from the    her face    mussels    so     he said
f.   It was coming out, growing from her face.  Mussels [too].  So he said,


41. "ŋ̓ənə?,     ʔə́y̓   kʷs    ƛ́áms.    skʷéy     kʷn̓s    yásu   )kʷəńtaɫχʷ
a.                                                       léŋətaɫxʷ.
m.   nom            dem-nom  -3sbj     nom as v  dem-2psv-nom  -pcl  -pur-1pobj
s.   voc       vi       subcl    vi        vi        subcl    vadv   vt
w.   child     it's good  that   it's o.k.  it's impos-  that   always   see us
w.             = it's enough          sible          you
f.   "Child, it's enough.   You can't always [come] see us.


42. ʔəw yás·xʷ      ʔəw ʔámət     ʔaɫ    ʔi?    kʷ    lé?esxʷ      qʷəqʷəw̓.
a.
m.       -2sbj              -ctv-                    -2sbj      ctv-
s.   pcl? vadv     pcl? vi         pcl    conj   dem?  vdem        vi
w.   you're always       sitting      just    and         you're     resting
w.                   = staying home              there
f.   You're always staying home and resting there.


43. yisá?s        kʷsu    ʔəw̓    skʷíwəɫ      yú?     ʔáwəná?   k̓ʷə
a. leŋítáɫxʷ                               ʔi-əw̓
m.( -3sbj)
m.(a) -pur-res-1pobj dem-nom-?   stat- -ctv-1psbj  conj-ctras  vneg=nom  dem
s.(vi)                           ctras
s.(a) vt impt       conj    pcl     vi                conj     vi      rlcl
w.(he said)
w.(a) look at us/     because      we're showing       and      there's  that's
w.(a)  watch us                                                  nothing
f.   Look at/watch us because we're showing and don't


44. šlé?es     kʷən̓    scecéyəkʷ.     ʔəw̓   xčítsən      kʷən̓    səw̓
a.
m.   nom-  -3sbj  dem-2psv  stat-              -pur-res-1ssbj  dem-2psv  nom-pcl
s.   vdem          rlcl     vi          ctras     vt           subcl     pcl
```

w. it's there that you worry   I know it   that you
f. worry about anything there. I know that you

45. ʔəsléleʔ   ʔə kʷ səns   kʷən̓   šléʔ.   níɬ
a.
m. stat-   indefdem vi dem-2psv   nom-
s. vadj   obl   indef nom   rlcl   vdem   vdem
w. are alright   wherever it is   that you are there   that's it
f. are alright where you're at when you're there.

46. wáʔače (ʔ)əw̓ kʷəns   txʷən̓étəŋ   kʷns   yiʔáx̣ʷ
a.
m. presum ctras dem-2psv-nom txʷ= 'toward'   dem-2psv-nom motion-
m.   -pur-res-pass-ctv
s. pcl   ctras   subcl   vt   relcl   vi
w. I guess   that you are being taken toward what you are going to
f. I guess that's the way you're being taken toward what you're going to

47. ʔə   kʷ   séʔenəŋ   sən   sčélə(ʔ)čeʔ.   láʔa   kʷəw̓
a.
m.   vi/vdemʔ-pass-ctvʔ dem-2psv -pl-   past   dem-pcl
s. obl   indef nom   dem-pron   nom   vaux   dem
w.   wherever they're at   your(f.)   relatives   ambig.past that
f. where you're relatives are at.

48. c̓əx̌ʷíŋətəxʷ.   x̣əɬáʔasts   ʔə cə ʔəw mák̓ʷstéŋ   sʔíɬən.
a.
m. -pur –3obj-2subsbj –ctv-caus- –3sbj   dem   pcl? vadj=vi   nom=
s.   vt   vt   obl art   vadj   nom
w. you've helped   he's feeding   the   everything/all food
w. them   them   = every kind of
f. You've helped them (your relatives).
f. He's feeding them every kind of food.

49. kʷéʔetaɬxʷ   skʷəče.   ʔiʔ   ʔíyəsəsxʷ   ʔaɬ kʷn̓s   léʔe
a.   /ʔəw̓
m.-pur-2pobj-impt expl   /ctras   -fut-2sbj pcl dem-2psv-nom
s.   vt   pcl   conj/pcl   vadj
w. (you can) leave us alone   and   you're going just   when you are
w.   /really   to be happy   there
f. [You can] leave us alone. And you're going to be happy when you're there

50. kʷs   yiƛíƛəč.   wəx̌ʷənéŋ   ʔaɬ ʔəce kʷənə   sƛíʔ."
a.   ʔiʔeƛíƛəč."   /sqʷéɬ. ʔəsə́p.
m. dem-nom motion-   wə- 'when'?   req   dem-1psv nom-

```
m.(a)                                                    nom-        stat-
s. rlcl        vadv          vi        pcl    pcl    rlcl
s.(a)                                                    nom         nrend
w. that's down below  that's all    just             that I   want
w.(a)                                                            /say      it's over
w.(a)                                                                      (of story)
f. down below.  That's all I want."
f.(a) down below."   That's all I('m going to) say.  It's over.
```

REFERENCES CITED

Bouchard, Randy

    1974   Classified Word List for B.C. Indian Languages, Straits (Saanich) Version. Victoria: B.C. Indian Language Project, unpubl. ms.

Chafe, Wallace L.

    1962   Estimates Regarding the Present Speakers of North American Indian Languages. International Journal of American Linguistics 28:162-171.

Charles, Al, Richard A. Demers and Elizabeth Bowman

    1978   Introduction to the Lummi Language. University of Arizona, Western Washington University, and Lummi Indian Reservation, unpubl. ms.

Demers, Richard A.

    1974   Alternating Roots in Lummi. International Journal of American Linguistics 40:15-21.

    1980a   The Category AUX in Lummi. A paper presented at the 15th International Conference on Salishan Languages, Vancouver, B.C.

    1980b   ?u? in Lummi. A handout circulated at the 1st Working Conference on Central Salish Languages, Vancouver, B.C.

    1982   Personal communication (Lummi cognates with Galloway 1982)

Efrat, Barbara S.

    1969   A Grammar of Non-particles in Sooke, a Dialect of Straits Coast Salish. Ph.D. dissertation, University of Pennsylvania, unpubl.

    ca 1980   The Interpretation of Glottalized Resonants in Straits Salish. In Linguistic and Literary Studies in Honor of A. A. Hill. M. A. Jazayery, E. Polomé and W. Winter. Lisse: Peter de Ridder Press.

Galloway, Brent D.

    1977   A Grammar of Chilliwack Halkomelem. Ph.D. dissertation, University of California at Berkeley, forthcoming in University of California Publications in Linguistics. Berkeley: University of California Press.

    1980   The Structure of Upriver Halq'eméylem, A Grammatical Sketch, and Classified Word List for Upriver Halq'eméylem. Sardis, B.C.: Coqualeetza Education Training Centre.

    1982   Proto-Central Salish Phonology and Sound Correspondences. A monograph presented in part at the 17th International Conference on Salishan Languages, Portland, Ore., unpubl.

Gibbs, George

    ca 1853-1860   Vocabularies, Washington Terr[itory]. Smithsonian Institution, Bureau of American Ethnology Manuscript Collection, Ms. #227.

Hukari, Thomas E.

    1981   Glottalization in Cowichan. Working Papers of the Linguistic Circle of the University of Victoria 1:233-250.

Jelinek, Eloise and Richard A. Demers

    1983   The Agent Hierarchy and Voice in Some Coast Salish Languages. International Journal of American Linguistics 49:167-185

Kennedy, Dorothy

    1974   Knowledge and Use of Fish by the Saanich (Straits Coast Salish) Indian People of Southeastern Vancouver Island, preliminary draft. Victoria: British Columbia Indian Language Project, unpubl. ms.

Kuipers, Aert

    1970   Towards a Salish Etymological Dictionary. Lingua 26:46-72.

    1982   Towards a Salish Etymological Dictionary II. Lingua 57:71-92.

Mitchell, Marjorie R.

    1968   A Dictionary of Songish, a Dialect of Straits Salish. M.A. thesis, University of Victoria, unpubl.

Montler, Timothy R.

    1984   Saanich Morphology and Phonology. Ph.D. dissertation, University of Hawaii at Manoa, [in press].

Pidgeon, Michael

    1970   Lexical Suffixes in Saanich, a Dialect of Straits Coast Salish. M.A. thesis, University of Victoria, unpubl.

Raffo, Yolanda A.

    1972   A Phonology and Morphology of Songish, a Dialect of Straits Salish. Ph.D. dissertation, University of Kansas, unpubl.

Seaburg, William R.

    1985   Stalking the Wild Pigeon: Diffusion of a Word for 'Pigeon' on the Northwest Coast. A paper presented at the 20th International Conference on Salish and Neighboring Languages, Vancouver, B.C., preprints:337-346.

Suttles, Wayne P.

    1951   Economic Life of the Coast Salish of Haro and Rosario Straits. Ph.D. dissertation, University of Washington, unpubl.

    1980   Fragments Relevant to Some Questions About Aspect from a Manuscript on the Musqueam Dialect of Halkomelem. Handout at the 1st Working Conference on Central Salish Languages, Vancouver, B.C.

Thompson, Laurence C.

    1972   Un cas de métaphonie en lummi. In Langues et techniques, nature et société, 1:257-260, Approche linguistique. Josephine M. C. Thomas and Lucien Bernot, eds. Paris: Klincksieck.

    1979   Salishan and the Northwest. In Native Languages of the Americas 1:359-425. Thomas A. Sebeok, ed. New York: Plenum Press.

Thompson, Laurence C. and M. Dale Kinkade

    Forthcoming   Linguistic Relations and Distributions. In Handbook of American Indians, vol. 7, The Northwest Coast. Wayne P. Suttles, ed.

Thompson, Laurence C. and M. Terry Thompson

    1971   Clallam, a Preview. In Studies in American Indian Languages, Univeristy of California Publications in Linguistics 65:251-294. Jesse Sawyer, ed.

Forthcoming   Thompson Salish Grammar.

Thompson, Laurence C., M. Terry Thompson, and Barbara S. Efrat

   1974   Some Phonological Developments in Straits Salish. International
     Journal of American Linguistics 40:182-196.

United States Census Bureau

   1880   10th Federal Population Census, Indian Division, Record Group 29,
     Microcopy T9, rolls 1397-8, families 76-106.

Canadian Museum of Civilization
Canadian Ethnology Service

Gratis

The following Canadian Ethnology Service
papers are available from:

Publications
Canadian Ethnology Service
Canadian Museum of Civilization
100 Laurier Street
P.O. Box 3100, Station B
Hull, Québec
J8X 4H2
Canada

Musée canadien des civilisations
Service canadien d'Ethnologie

Gratuit

On peut obtenir les dossiers suivants du
Service canadien d'Ethnologie de:

Publications
Service canadien d'Ethnologie
Musée canadien des civilisations
100, rue Laurier
C.P. 3100, Succursale B
Hull (Québec)
J8X 4H2
Canada

1   PRELIMINARY STUDY OF TRADITIONAL KUTCHIN CLOTHING by Judy Thompson (1972).
    92 pages.

2   SARCEE VERB PARADIGMS by Eung-Do Cook (1972). 51 pages.

3   GAMBLING MUSIC OF THE COAST SALISH INDIANS by Wendy Boss Stuart (1972).
    114 pages.

6   INKONZE. Magico Religious Beliefs of Contact-Traditional Chipewyan at Fort
    Resolution, N.W.T. by David Merrill Smith (1973). 21 pages.

7   THE MIDDLE GROUND: Social Change in an Arctic Community, 1967-71 by Joel S.
    Savishinsky and Susan B. Frimmer (1973). 54 pages, 1 map, 2 figures,
    2 tables.

10 PAPERS IN LINGUISTICS FROM 1972 CONFERENCE ON IROQUOIAN RESEARCH, ed. by
    M.K. Foster (1974). 118 pages.

11 MUSEOCINEMATOGRAPHY: Ethnographic Film Programs of the National Museum of
    Man, 1913-73 by D.W. Zimmerly (1974). 103 pages, 22 figures.

13 RIDING ON THE FRONTIERS CREST: Mahican Indian Culture and Culture Change by
    T.J. Brasser (1974). 91 pages, 5 plates, 1 map.

16 AN EVALUATIVE ETHNO-HISTORICAL BIBLIOGRAPHY OF THE MALECITE INDIANS by
    M. Harrison (1974). 260 pages.

17 PROCEEDINGS OF THE FIRST CONGRESS OF THE CANADIAN ETHNOLOGY SOCIETY ed. by
    J.H. Barkow (1974). 226 pages.

18   KOYUKUK RIVER CULTURE by A. McFadyen Clark (1974).   282 pages, 5 maps.

23   PAPERS OF THE SIXTH ALGONQUIAN CONFERENCE, 1974 ed. by W. Cowan (1975).
     399 pages.

26   A PLACE OF REFUGE FOR ALL TIME: Migration of the American Potawatomi into
     Upper Canada 1830-50 by J.A. Clifton (1975).   152 pages, 3 maps, 7 plates.

42   A PRACTICAL DICTIONARY OF THE COAST TSIMSHIAN LANGUAGE by John Asher Dunn
     (1978).   155 pages.

66   THE INUIT LANGUAGE IN SOUTHERN LABRADOR FROM 1694 TO 1785/LA LANGUE INUIT AU
     SUD DU LABRADOR DE 1694 À 1785 by/par Louis-Jacques Dorais (1980).   56 pages,
     1 map/1 carte.

70   ANALYSE LINGUISTIQUE ET ETHNOCENTRISME: Essai sur la structure du mot en
     Inuktitut par Ronald Lowe (1981).

79   MUSICAL TRADITIONS OF THE LABRADOR COAST INUIT by Maija M. Lutz (1982).
     89 pages, 2 maps, 1 table.

80   NORTH-WEST RIVER (SHESHATSHIT) MONTAGNAIS: A Grammatical Sketch by Sandra
     Clarke (1982).   185 pages.

81   MOOSE-DEER ISLAND HOUSE PEOPLE: A History of the Native People of Fort
     Resolution by David M. Smith (1982).   202 pages, 1 table, 3 figures, 10 maps.

82   MUSIC OF THE NETSILIK ESKIMO: A Study of Stability and Change, Volumes I and
     II by Beverly Cavanagh (1982).   570 pages, 16 figures, 10 plates, 1 vinyl
     record.

84   OOWEKEENO ORAL TRADITIONS: As Told by the Late Chief Simon Walkus Sr.
     Transcribed and translated by Evelyn Walkus Windsor.   Edited by Susanne
     Hilton and John Rath (1982).   223 pages, 2 maps.

86   THE MUSICAL LIFE OF THE BLOOD INDIANS by Robert Witmer (1982).   185 pages.

87   THE STOLEN WOMAN: Female Journeys in Tagish and Tutchone Narratives by Julie
     Cruikshank (1982).   131 pages.

88   AN ETHNOHISTORIC STUDY OF EASTERN JAMES BAY CREE SOCIAL ORGANIZATION, 1700-
     1850 by Toby Morantz (1983).   199 pages, 6 tables, 4 maps.

89E CONSCIOUSNESS AND INQUIRY: Ethnology and Canadian Realities.   Edited by
     Frank Manning (1983).   365 pages.

89F CONSCIENCE ET ENQUÊTE: L'ethnologie des réalitiés canadiennes.   Marc-Adélard
     Tremblay, rédacteur (1983).   407 pages.

90   AN OJIBWA LEXICON.   Edited by G.L. Piggott and A. Grafstein (1983).
     377 pages.

91   MICMAC LEXICON by Albert D. DeBlois and Alphonse Metallic (1983).   392 pages.

92   THE BELLA COOLA LANGUAGE by H.F. Nater (1983). 170 pages.

93   COAST SALISH GAMBLING GAMES by Lynn Maranda (1984). 143 pages.

96   BEAR LAKE ATHAPASKAN KINSHIP AND TASK GROUP FORMATION by Scott Rushforth
        (1984). 204 pages, 11 figures, 16 tables.

97   EDWARD SAPIR'S CORRESPONDENCE: An Alphabetical and Chronological Inventory,
        1910-25. Edited by Louise Dallaire (1984). 278 pages.

98   INTERPRETIVE CONTEXTS FOR TRADITIONAL AND CURRENT COAST TSIMSHIAN FEASTS by
        Margaret Seguin (1985). 114 pages, 2 maps, 1 table, 2 figures.

100   THE RED EARTH CREES, 1860-1960 by David Meyer (1985). 231 pages, 5 tables,
        24 figures, 21 plates.

102   BEOTHUK BARK CANOES: An Analysis and Comparative Study by Ingeborg Constanze
        Luise Marshall (1985). 159 pages, 34 figures, 11 tables, 1 map.

PE3   FAMILLE ET PARENTÉ EN ACADIE par M.A. Tremblay (1971). 174 pages, 5 annexes,
        47 tables.

PE5   THE QUEST FOR FOOD AND FURS: The Mistassini Cree, 1953-54 by E.S. Rogers
        (1973). 83 pages, 17 plates, 7 figures, 6 tables, 9 maps, 7 graphs.

PE8   THE "MOTS LOUPS" OF FATHER MATHEVET by G.M. Day (1975).

PE9   LABRADOR ESKIMO SETTLEMENTS OF THE EARLY CONTACT PERIOD by J.G. Taylor
        (1974). 105 pages, 1 figure, 26 tables, 4 maps.

B138   BELLE-ANSE by M. Rioux (1957). 125 pages.

B176H   THE LYNX POINT PEOPLE: The Dynamics of a Northern Athapaskan Band by J. Helm
        (1961). 193 pages, 8 figures, 6 tables. Hard cover.

B176S   THE LYNX POINT PEOPLE: The Dynamics of a Northern Athapaskan Band by J. Helm
        (1961). 193 pages, 8 figures, 6 tables. Soft cover.

B179H   BAND ORGANIZATION OF THE PEEL RIVER KUTCHIN by R. Slobodin (1962). 97 pages,
        4 plates, 3 figures, 2 maps. Hard cover.

B179S   BAND ORGANIZATION OF THE PEEL RIVER KUTCHIN by R. Slobodin (1962). 97 pages,
        4 plates, 3 figures, 2 maps. Soft cover.

CER1   MYTHS AND TRADITIONS FROM NORTHERN ALASKA, THE MACKENZIE DELTA AND CORONATION
        GULF by D. Jenness (1924). 90 pages.

CER2   COMPARATIVE VOCABULARY OF THE WESTERN ESKIMO DIALECTS by D. Jenness (1928).
        134 pages.